Praise for

The Map Is Not the Journey

"If your spirit is weary or your faith is running dry, this book is like a refreshing drink from an alpine spring. It will take you above the tree line of discouragement and help you renew your enthusiasm and rekindle your joy. You'll find yourself walking in Richard's boots as he paints incredible word pictures and takes you on a compelling journey of transformation. Breathe deep and take it in. A truly inspiring book for everyone who seeks renewed motivation and deeper meaning."

—**Les Parrott, PhD,** *New York Times* best-selling author of *The Good Fight*

"I'm deeply grateful for Richard's musings on the journey of life. It's as if he was writing directly to me, talking about how journeys define our lives, warning about the dangers of success, reminding that our packs can get too full, that control is an illusion, and how the greater dangers are usually the subtle ones. And then to hit us with, 'God. Is. Enough.' Impactful!"

—**Mike Romberger,** President/CEO, Mount Hermon Christian Conference Center

"Richard Dahlstrom's travels and adventures in the Alps aren't just good stories of adventure in far-away places. Though told well enough to bring me right into the Alps with him, they're also instructive on how unexpected everyday experiences can shape us to become better people. Those looking to find God in the commonplace will benefit from this book."

—**Jim Zorn,** long-time NFL player and coach. "Go Hawks." Proverbs 22:1

"Whenever I can, I sneak over to Richard Dahlstrom's church, where I am not a member, just to hear his amazing insights. He writes in this book about the burnout that can come after a long obedience in the same direction. He speaks to the 'world worn' and the weary. But if you trek with Richard through these chapters, you might rediscover the joy of serving God afresh."

—**Richard Stearns,** President of World Vision U.S. and author of *The Hole in Our Gospel* and *Unfinished*

"For those feeling fatigue after years of faithfully doing the same thing, for those looking for new eyes to see what God is doing and has on his mind, and for those who need a jolt of adventure, this is the book to read."

—**Denny Rydberg,** President Emeritus, Young Life

"I like this book! I like the way Richard, with considerable input from his wife Donna, has told a story about the day-by-day experience of an alpine trek. The fifteen chapters are a mixture of all important details describing the Alps, along with inner soul reflections about Richard's personal faith journey, favorite texts from the Bible, pastoral mandate, and his, sometimes self-punishing, reflections. The narrative is believable, the people they meet are sensitively described, and there is the scenery of the Alps too. I liked this book very much."

—**Earl F. Palmer,** former Senior Pastor, University Presbyterian Church in Seattle and Director, Earl Palmer Ministries

"Richard guides us through his journey in the Alps and opens our eyes to God's heart for all of us. I couldn't wait to be brought into the next scene and hear how God had transformed his earthly adventure into an eternal truth. This book gave insight into my personal journey as well as how I lead those traveling with me."

—**Mike Gaffney,** Vice-President, YoungLife College and University Ministry

THE MAP IS NOT THE

JOURNEY

THE MAP IS NOT THE

JOURNEY

Faith Renewed while Hiking the Alps

RICHARD DAHLSTROM

LEAFWOOD
P U B L I S H E R S
an imprint of Abilene Christian University Press

THE MAP IS NOT THE JOURNEY
Faith Renewed while Hiking the Alps

LEAFWOOD
P U B L I S H E R S
an imprint of Abilene Christian University Press

Copyright © 2017 by Richard Dahlstrom

ISBN 978-0-89112-526-6 | LCCN 2017040014

Printed in the United States of America

Published in association with MacGregor Agency, Manzanita, Oregon.

LIBRARY OF CONGRESS CATALOGING-IN-PUBLICATION DATA
Names: Dahlstrom, Richard, 1956- author.
Title: The map is not the journey : faith renewed while hiking the Alps / Richard Dahlstrom.
Description: Abilene, Texas : Leafwood Publishers, 2017.
Identifiers: LCCN 2017040014 | ISBN 9780891125266 (pbk.)
Subjects: LCSH: Dahlstrom, Richard, 1956- | Christian biography. | Mountaineering—Alps. | Success—Religious aspects—Christianity.
Classification: LCC BR1725.D325 A3 2017 | DDC 263/.0424947—dc23
LC record available at https://lccn.loc.gov/201704001 4

Cover design by ThinkPen Design, Inc.
Interior text design by Sandy Armstrong, Strong Design

Leafwood Publishers is an imprint of Abilene Christian University Press
ACU Box 29138, Abilene, Texas 79699

1-877-816-4455 | www.leafwoodpublishers.com

ACKNOWLEDGMENTS

Just as the solo mountaineer is never truly a soloist, it's equally true that no author ever writes alone. So I offer my gratitude at the outset to the many people who made this work possible:

To Bethany Community Church:
Thank you for the generous gift of a sabbatical! A time freed from normal obligations and constraints is a rare gift in this world. That this gift has come from your commitment to me overwhelms me with gratitude.

To the Bethany Community Church Staff:
Every day I was gone you proved that the work of Christ is greater than any one of us. The faithful use of your gifts in my absence taught me in a powerful way that the church is, indeed, a body. When one member is resting, other members take up the work. Your "above and beyond," demonstrated daily in so many ways, was felt even more so during my time away. Thank you!

To Chip MacGregor of MacGregor Literary:
Thank you for long conversations in Seattle restaurants, for engaging theological discussions, and for your relentless belief in this project. I'm privileged to count you as friend, even more than agent!

To the Torchbearer Community:
Thank you for your collective passion to pour into the lives of young people, decade after decade, to the end that they will scatter throughout the world as nothing less than the presence of the risen Jesus, who in them has found hearts

willing to be shaped and used by him. Your modeling of that foundational truth remains as the glue that holds us together. May our ministry remain faithful to that mission for many decades to come.

To Tauernhof and Martin:
Thank you for providing space to write after our trek was over. Your hospitality, friendship, and kindred love of the mountains are priceless gifts in my life. I look forward to many more hours of spirited conversation in the years ahead!

Finally, to Donna:
Without you, who knows? Perhaps I'd never have grown to love the outdoors at all, for it was your effusive joy, from our very first hike together thirty-eight years ago, that made me want to #optoutside over and over again with you. Thank you for being my companion, my editor, my comedian, and the one through whom I see Christ's heart of love, service, and generosity so very clearly. Next time, let's take a couple of years and do the whole Via Alpina!

TABLE OF CONTENTS

OUR JOURNEYS DEFINE US

There's a hearing. It comes to us in dreams, or songs, or after a conversation in the corner booth on a Tuesday night with the one we love. Or maybe at a graveside, or a hospital, or in the wake of infidelity. However it comes to us, we hear the voice calling, beckoning.

There's a wrestling with what we've heard. Was it the wine or divinity? Am I responding to the weakness that makes me easily unsatisfied, or to the strength that I'm willing to risk it all—to shoot the moon in pursuit of a better story? We struggle to discern between the Siren calls of temptation and the tug of the divine, to have the courage to say yes or no. This is where wisdom is learned.

There's a response. Sometimes the response includes the creating of lists as we catalog the possible rewards and losses should we undertake the journey. We pray. We consult. We listen to our dreams more intently than ever. Then we go. Or stay. Whichever way we decide, it will make all the difference.

There's a preparation. If we're going, certain things will have to be done, so that already—even before we step outside the house—our priorities have changed. We're reading up on alpine travel instead of watching TV, saving up and buying what we'll need, getting in shape so that we can handle it, learning skills, and finding our life pruned and richer for the less that it's become.

There's a leaving. At some point, after we're prepped and packed, nothing is left to do except walk out the front door. And whether it's for a weekend getaway, or for the last time, or for God-only-knows-how-long in between, this moment—this nanosecond of turning away from the familiar—is a vital necessity. Although we're told we can have it all, we know in this instant that this assurance is rubbish. Now we know that we can't live in the now and still hold on to yesterday.

Click. The door is closed. *The Journey begins.*

Our journeys define our lives, because the best lives have movement of some sort—physical, spiritual, geographical, and emotional—as we walk through valleys of doubt and grief, ascend peaks of prosperity and health, know the warmth of intimacy, the cold of rejection, or the fog of isolation. Through all of it, learning to navigate, to take a step and move or stay put, and knowing when to do one or the other will change us forever.

Instead of living with intention and purpose, too many of us let the journey that is our lives just happen to us. If we do this, we wake up near the end and wonder what took place. Something's missing, and we don't even know what it is. Better to mind the gap between our longings and reality earlier in life while we still have time to make adjustments.

This book is about life journeys and about adjustments made, told through the lens of lessons learned as I ascended mountain peaks and descended through fog into misty river valleys, trekking hundreds of kilometers one summer with my wife of thirty-five years.

Here's what happened . . .

SECTION ONE

HEARING

ACCIDENTAL CLIMBERS

Many of us learn to do our "survival dance," but we never get to our actual "sacred dance."

—Richard Rohr

Success is a lousy teacher. It seduces smart people into thinking they can't lose.

—Bill Gates

Woe to you, when all people speak well of you.

—Jesus the Christ (Luke 6:26 ESV)

15

If success is a mountain, I'm an accidental climber.

Has it ever happened to you? You've been working hard for goals you believe in for a long time. You've sacrificed and said no to trinkets so that you could focus on the gold of your objectives, your future. It didn't happen overnight, but slowly, over time, it came to pass. You took initial steps into the unknown of a new job. Or you committed more deeply to some visionary idea, and the universe rewarded with you success. The business grew. You were promoted. The publisher said yes.

It feels good, so you stay on the path a little longer, and you continue to get a few more responsibilities. All the while, other areas of your life also begin to grow. You're a spouse now, maybe, or a parent, or you have a loan for a house and are slowly filling it with stuff. Your hard drive's filling up with pictures of kids at Christmas, Little League, prom night, and graduations. It's not perfect. You hit some bumps along the way, but you're getting more these days. Life's filling up. The business is gaining new market share. Investments are doing their job. It's all paying off.

Days become decades, quickly. Now there's money in the bank, and when the car breaks down, you don't worry about whether you can afford to get it fixed. You eat out a bit more, maybe a lot more. Others, looking in on your life from the outside, are a little envious, or maybe resentful. That's because you've become what our culture tells us is most important—in some measure at least, you've become "successful." You just kept walking, step by step, and eventually you found yourself high up on the slope by your own measure of fame or influence or upward mobility, looking down on the lights below. Pausing to look around for a moment, you wonder how you got here.

Once you have a little time to catch your breath, you look around, but nothing looks familiar. You're not sure where you are anymore. You thought this was the right path because back down there along the way everyone applauded and affirmed every step you took—college degree, corporate job, promotion, partner, consultant, marriage, kids, CrossFit, commute. The world's filled with cheerleaders ready to affirm or punish every step of the way so that the well-trodden mountain becomes your mountain too. You followed the path, almost without questioning, and now that you're up here, somewhere near the top, you're not sure this is where you belong.

That's because you like it here on the one hand, but on the other hand, getting here has taken a toll. You're tired, and the pace of life has become more like a video game, with obligations coming at you faster and faster so that you're reacting more than living. Things have become complicated, too, with some debts and a new lifestyle to which you've become accustomed. High up here on the mountain, a fall would be costly. There's your influence to consider, and your reputation. You need a little time to get your bearings before you proceed, but odds are you won't push for the needed time off unless something huge shakes you awake and forces you to ask questions you maybe should have asked years ago. But right then you were too busy succeeding to actually consider whether you were climbing the right mountain.

Just such a moment came my way last summer. I'd come home from two packed months of speaking at conferences on both coasts and in Europe, ending this season with a cross-country flight on a Friday night. At eight the next morning, I joined staff members of the church I lead to conduct round-robin interviews for four hours with several candidates for a single staff position. After these meetings were finished and I was having lunch with one of the candidates, my phone rang. "Germany?" I said to myself, seeing the +49 country code. Because I have a daughter there, I picked it up.

"Kristi! Good to hear from you . . ."

Silence. And then, "Richard, it's Peter."

"Peter. I thought you were Kristi. Listen, I'll call you back, I'm right in the middle of . . ."

"Nope. I need to chat now, for a just a minute or two." I walk away from the outdoor table just as the waiter brings our food. I'm sitting in rare Seattle sunshine by the front door of the restaurant when he says, "Hans Peter died today in the Alps. Paragliding. They found his body early this evening. I'll let you know more when I know the time of the funeral." After a silent moment, Peter says, "I know. I'm sick too." We chat a moment before I end the call and finish the perfunctory interview, wondering why the world hasn't stopped for everyone else on this outdoor patio, because God knows it has utterly collapsed for me. I can't eat, can't throw up, though I want to. Then I go home and sit in the sun that set hours ago in Austria, sinking behind the Alps and leaving a family I love reeling in darkness.

Hans Peter was the director of a school in the Alps where I teach regularly. He was a kindred spirit. We'd skied his mountains together there, snowshoed mine east of Seattle, and ridden bikes amongst the monuments of Washington, DC. We'd rejoiced and agonized over our kids, argued theology, and commiserated about leadership. We'd walked life together enough that although we were separated by six thousand miles or so, he was one of my best friends. And now he was gone.

The next day, I broke down while telling my congregation this devastating news, but on Monday there was an important retreat to lead for my marvelous staff. It would be filled with laughter and adventures, and I just kept pushing, because there was always another thing to do just around the corner. The retreat ended, and I sat in a stream and talked at a camera for a video that needed making. Then home again, then studying for Sunday, then preaching three times.

After that, I collapsed. For a day or two, the thought of getting out of bed to make a little coffee was overwhelming. Actually doing my job was out of the question. The convergence of weariness and loss created a crisis of introspection that forever changed my life.

Walking alone in the mountains, I thought about how I'd succeeded at the things I'd gone after during the past two decades—teaching, preaching, leading, investing in others, writing. It was all good stuff, not some pyramid scheme or an attempt to make a quick killing in the market so I could "hit the beach." We're talking about meaningful work that I enjoyed and that had in some sense "prospered." But somehow, the convergence of my weariness and my friend's death opened the door to an intense looking inward, and I began to wonder if I was doing the right thing, if the hamster wheel of activity was meaningful after all.

Was it weariness I was feeling, or was it the work itself that was broken? Big churches, defined by everyone around them as inherently successful, were suddenly up for a thorough evaluation, something I'd not done before because I'd never cared about growth or success—or so I told myself. Was I telling myself the truth all those years, or was it a cover for ambition? What's next? Can I keep doing this, and for how long? I had questions, but when I looked around, all I saw was the fog of weariness. I wondered if I was on the right mountain.

Later that fall I went to some sort of seminar for pastors of big churches and, though I participated outwardly, I felt like a stranger at the table. Everyone was excited about their plans, goals, mission statements, "strategies for staff alignment." Even their challenges were energizing to them. I felt disembodied some of the time, more like an observer than a participant. What was wrong with me? As the day wore on and I considered the dissonance between their excitement and my relative apathy, I began to think that I was suffering from the fruit of my own success.

I'd climbed the mountain of ambition, so to speak, and though I'd enjoyed most of the steps along the way, the climb was tiring. As on any peak, reaching the top came at a cost. Now, at fifty-eight, just when I was beginning to think the mountain would level out toward a plateaued summit, I was getting busier than ever because the work I was leading was still growing. New locations. New leaders. New responsibilities. New team chemistry because continually adding people to the team was changing our roles and relationships. The whole thing was my vision; it was working; it was exciting. But it had taken on a life of its own, and I was on Empty, having used up all the creative fuel in the pursuit as growth, opportunities, and challenges piled on top of each other, year after year.

Success! And emptiness at the same time. Should I continue climbing this mountain, or might there be another?

When you're young, nobody tells you about the dangers of success. Success is like a disco ball, high up there on the ceiling in the center of the room, and all the lights of everyone's ambitions are shining on it, so that its beauty is magnified as it reflects with sparkle back to everyone in the room the collective pursuits of greatness, as if to say, "This is what it's all about." You want it to shine on you, too.

We call it lots of things, depending on our profession. We want to build great teams, provide service second to none, create a product everyone needs, cure cancer, end human trafficking, write the song, get the corner office, get into Sundance, make the *New York Times* Bestseller List, raise amazing kids, find true love. Let's face it, there's a gold medal in every area of life. Maybe this isn't a bad thing. After all, we all need a reason to get up in the morning. We want our lights to shine. We want significance. I get it.

Conventional Wisdom, or any disguise dressed as the same, capitalizes on these longings for success. That's what seminars are for, and books about losing one hundred pounds, or running marathons, or creating a marketing strategy. An entire "pursuit of success" industry flourishes precisely because we believe that "going after it" is the right thing to do, and maybe it is.

I'd always thought I wasn't in that camp. In a world of BIG, I'd made my living running a church in my living room and teaching at tiny Bible schools around the world several weeks a year. In a world of urban, I was living with my wife and three children in a place where the phone book was a single sheet of paper. We were rural, small, subsistence. We had resource challenges at times, but even though we lived below the poverty line, we slept under the stars on clear nights, camped in old fire lookouts where Jack Kerouac spent his summers, and enjoyed tiny staff meetings around the kitchen table. It was hard work, and frugal, lacking notoriety, but life-giving.

Then, when opportunity came knocking, I answered. We moved to the city where I would lead what, to my mind, was an enormous church of three hundred people. "Teaching is teaching," I said naively, believing that the practice of my craft would be the same whether the place was large or small. I was wrong, of course. Bigger stuff is more complex than small stuff, and though that is self-evident to most people, it wasn't clear to me. I needed to learn it firsthand, as our big church started to grow even bigger.

Growth wasn't the goal, but health was, and the reality is that if people are healthy in spirit, their joy, generosity, hearts of service, capacity to survive trials, and willingness to cross social divides will attract more people, just as moths are drawn to flame. In this terribly needy world, I believe that people are hungry for community, meaning, and for living in a better story than the pursuit of self-fulfillment. When people are looking for this kind of life and find others seeking it too—even living it in some measure—they will be attracted to it and be drawn in.

That's what started happening, and it happened for nearly two decades, slowly and steadily. This growth meant adding staff, adding buildings, saying goodbye to staff for whom the change and growth weren't right, dealing with changing team dynamics, altering organization charts, creating new positions, reorganizing structures and systems to accommodate "bigger," adding new locations so that we could offer the same kind of healthy community in other neighbor-hoods, raising funds, dealing with complexities that happen when competing visions and ideologies sneak in under this larger umbrella, facing the rejection of those who don't like change and the adulation of those who do (both equally dangerous), and so much more. HR task forces. Policy manuals. Bigger and bigger budgets. Adapt. Grow. Celebrate. Adapt. Grow. Mourn a little bit. Celebrate. Repeat.

People began writing to me wondering "how we did it," and the truth is that I didn't know, because I wasn't trying to do it at all. I was simply trying to create a healthy community and build systems that could help others join while still remaining healthy. After we built our new building, I received a magazine in the mail congratulating me that our church had made the list of the "100 Fastest Growing Churches in America." I didn't even know that anyone was keeping score, but here we were, on the coveted "list." Year after year, it was the same, whether we were adding buildings, or locations, or lead-ers: Growth. The growth, of course, represented much more than added people; it represented changed people. Healed. Empowered. Transformed. Not everyone, that's for certain, but many.

I knew I should be happy about this, but after about our sixteenth year of continual growth, I began to ask, "Where does this story end?" And the honest answer was that I didn't know. This is because some-times the only picture of success we can see is the single disco ball in the room. The commonly held metrics of achievement are, in truth, surprisingly few, and predictable. "Growth"—whether of sales, souls, or influence—is the low-hanging fruit, the easy way to convince our-selves that we're significant.

Lots of people go after this low-hanging fruit, some with gusto and unapologetic clarity. Others stumble into it by simply doing their jobs well. But whatever our on-ramp, it's all the same: we're heading toward the disco ball in hope that *our* light will be magnified. And now, here I was staring into the multifaceted light of success, and I realized I couldn't see a thing. I didn't know where I was or where I was heading. What I did know was that this kind of success had created an environment where the complexity of the machinery seemed to be consuming too much of my creative energy, leaving me running on Empty. When that happens, we can't see far enough ahead to lead well, we can't parse our motives with any sort of clarity, we can't contribute what is life-giving to others and ourselves. Like thin air in the high mountains, this is not a place to stay for long. I knew I needed to move.

I asked my board for three months off so that I could get off the treadmill, get my bearings, and return, not only with a sense of refreshment, but with a recalibrated soul, better able to serve, lead, and discern the signs. Little did I know that I was on the cusp of an important journey I thought I'd never take.

Richard Rohr reminds us that in Homer's *Odyssey,* the oft-forgotten part of the story is the final two chapters. The major story has to do with Odysseus coming home from war and all that he encountered along the way, overcoming trials and temptations in order to be united with his wife, son, and old dear father. Here's what Rohr says about what happens next:

> Accustomed as we are to our normal storyline, we rightly
> expect a "happily ever after" ending to Odysseus's tale.
> And for most readers, that is all, in fact, they need, want,
> or remember from the story. . . . (But) in the final two
> chapters, after what seems like a glorious and appropriate
> ending, Homer announces and calls Odysseus to a
> new and second journey that is barely talked about, yet
> somehow Homer deemed it absolutely necessary to his
> character's life.[1]

We get high up on the mountain of success, looking for a plateau where we can settle and bask in the glories of our achievements. We think that the goal is "up there" somewhere, in the land of more. Instead, I found an invitation to take a path down, out of speed and into slow, out of complexity and into simplicity, out of comfort and into suffering, out of certainty and into dependency. I found an invitation to walk down a path that would shake me awake, challenging me literally every step of the way. I found an invitation to hit the pause button on the dangerous, if not toxic, treadmill of spiritual success in search of something that I had once, but which had slipped away. The convergence of my weariness born from success and the death of my friend pointed me toward the path of getting out from behind my books and desk and out of my car, alone, away from the crowds, and putting one foot in front of the other for hundreds of miles, from Canada to California on the Pacific Crest Trail. In the course of doing so, my hope was to recalibrate, discovering once again the freshness and joy that were my life of faith in earlier days

And so it was that my wife and I began planning a hike together through the Alps.

Note

[1]Richard Rohr, *Falling Upward: A Spirituality for the Two Halves of Life* (San Francisco: Joseph-Bass Publishing, 2011), xxii.

DECISIONS AND THEIR ROOTS

CHAPTER TWO

In their hearts humans plan their course,
but the LORD establishes their steps.
—Proverbs 16:9 NIV

There is no story without a journey, and no journey without
adventures, and no adventures in perpetual success.
—Cosmin Andron

The thing that was so profound to me that summer—
and yet also, like most things, so very simple—
was how few choices I had.
—Cheryl Strayed

July 25. Remote alpine region in Styria, Austria.[1] *Rain spits intermittently from the sky. I'm standing in the middle of a forest high in the Alps. A blend of silver fir, pine, and larch have created a sanctuary punctuated by large mossy boulders strewn about. We're near the edge of tree line, where the terrain above is rocky with a bit of moss, or higher still, just rock. There's a small clearing, and fifty people, students and staff of a small school, are just finishing lunch. They're a patchwork quilt of multicolored Gore-Tex, mostly jackets, with a few ponchos as seasoning. From all over Europe and North America, along with one from Chile, they have just come down from above tree line, so they're wet, cold, hungry. It's the last week of their five-week Alps experience, and the whole of it has been more cloud than sun, more wet than dry.*

I don't know them. Having just arrived from Seattle, I hiked up this morning after a great night's sleep and a full breakfast. They munch what little food they have left at the end of their multiday hike, mostly in silence, and it's hard to read whether they're sullen or just tired. My friend who runs this program gathers everyone around and introduces me. "We have a very special guest for our last week of Bible School, a pastor from Seattle who also teaches a great deal with us here in Austria and . . ." Etcetera. I feel that nervous excitement some of us who speak feel just before it's time to open our mouths, only more so in this instance because of the challenges of speaking to a hungry, soggy group of people

I've never met. Outdoors. In the rain. These mountains, these students, this teaching—none of it was in the plan when I proposed a sabbatical break. What happened?

Have you noticed that some of our most consequential decisions—some of the choices we make that change our lives the most—happen almost without our realizing that options are being approved or rejected? I hadn't traveled much in my life until 1993, when I was invited to a gathering of leaders in the "Torchbearer"[2] community at Capernwray Hall, an old estate in the Lakes District of Northern England purchased after WWII by a British major with a vision of providing hospitality and teaching to young adults to the end that they might know Jesus in a real way rather than just a religious one. The leaders of Torchbearers, a fellowship of study centers scattered across five continents, gather every four years to conduct business and to see that the work they belong to is bigger than any of their single local expressions. "The sun never sets on torchbearing," as their saying goes. It's a way of declaring that the light of Christ is shining around the globe through these scattered folk. I was thrilled to join up with them for the meetings in England back then. Because I've been involved in small independent churches my whole career, they'd become my theological family. I'd begun traveling and teaching at a few of the centers, and the friendships formed with staff and leaders by returning year after year had become a great gift.

England in 1993 meant the chance to meet still more of this community, beyond the North American centers where I'd taught. It was there I met the staff of the school in Austria, there that Hans Peter and I first met and spoke of our sons (we each had one) and daughters (we each had two), and of parenting, mountains, ministry. We both spoke at the conference, and shortly after that, I was invited to Austria to teach, a pilgrimage that has happened nearly every year for the past twenty. Those weeks in Austria would be marked by a deepening friendship between Hans Peter and me, as our children grew into adulthood, mine visiting Austria, his son visiting Seattle to ski with mine. Lives intermingled. Questions pondered. Mountains climbed together on both our continents. Friendship. These things are a sweetness of life.

The Alps Invitation

Days after my Austrian friend died, I was chatting with someone in Seattle who said, "They'll call you. They'll need your help." I didn't think anything of it at the time, but a few weeks later, the new director of the school in Austria did call. It became apparent that I could help by coming over and teaching a bit because of the vacuum that had been left by losing Hans Peter. Martin, who had already been running the Bible School there before this tragedy, was already in line for becoming the director, just not this soon.

I looked at Martin, the quintessential Austrian, on my tiny phone screen. "Yes. As it happens, I have some extended time off this coming summer and would be happy to help." The center runs a five-week English-speaking program integrating rock climbing, hiking, river rafting, orienteering, and caving with teaching from the Bible so that truths which often hang aimlessly in the atmosphere as dry-bones theology have a better chance to take root in the soil of souls and flower into life transformation. It's a marvelous way to invest a piece of life, but summers have always been full at home, so I've never visited the Alps to teach in the summer.

This year, though? Three months are blocked out as empty, roughly divided into a chunk for hiking, and the remainder for rest and learning. Alps? Pacific Crest Trail? The decision is ultimately made based on friendship more than geography, on the desire to contribute in some small way to a tiny community tucked away in the Alps that I'd come to love, a work to which I'd been committed for more than two decades. "I can help this summer, and in the fall too," I said. Just like that, the Alps became my destination. This little change of geography would change everything, even before I took a single step.

The mountains of the American west are wild by any standard, but especially in contrast to the highly developed routes in the Alps, which date back to the Roman Empire, and even earlier. Hiking the Pacific Crest Trail from California to Canada entails carrying your shelter, food, fuel, and cookstove on your back. Freeze-dried food and chunks of beef jerky are typically mailed to various postal outlets in proximity to the chosen route. Highways run east/west into and through these mountains, and the trail runs north/south along the crest of the mountains, so that every sixty or eighty or forty miles, you reach a highway, walk or hitchhike to a general store and/or post-office, and pick up your stash of power bars and freeze-dried meals you mailed to yourself before you began. This food being our lifeline, and bears being hungry too, we hikers out west have rituals related to hanging our food high in trees, in bags, at the end of a long rope so that it's still available when we wake up, rather than eaten by the creatures who call the wilderness home.

The Alps, on the other hand, have created a culture of mountain huts that are heavily favored over tent camping. The notion of a "hut" might evoke images of sheet metal shelters and half-crazed hikers shivering in thick down bags as they fight over the last shreds of oatmeal. Huts in the Alps are not that. Not at all. At one of our first huts, we walked inside out of a biting wind to a dining area warmed by a wood stove with light jazz playing. People sat around eating steaming plates of pasta while they pored over maps and discussed planned routes from here to other huts in various directions. Our host greeted us with a glass of peach Schnapps, and we knew immediately we weren't on the Pacific Crest Trail. It's a culture of trekking unfamiliar to Americans but well-established in Europe. The lavishness of the shelter makes hiking far more accessible there than in our American West. I joined the British Division of the Austrian Alpine Club in order both to get educated about the process and to enjoy the privileges of priority reservations and specially discounted "mountaineers meals."

Another distinction between our mountain cultures is options. The American West Coast has just one big trail if you're planning something epic, perhaps because we've settled in the place just about one heartbeat ago in the history of humankind. The Alps, on the other hand, have a massive crisscross of trails that will let you begin nearly anywhere in one of the eight countries they occupy and hike to anywhere else, or beyond anywhere else. There's a trail called the "Via Claudia Augustine" (named after the Roman emperor who established it just before Jesus was born). There's the E2 trail heading north/south from England to the bottom of France, or the E4, an east/west throughway from Spain to Greece. You can start in Munich and end in Venice, or take Jacob's Way through the length of Austria. "Where in Europe do you want to go today?" There's a trail that will take you there. Variety. Comfort. Ease of access. And for meals? How about the beverage of your choice, pasta so perfect it had to have been prepared in heaven, and strudel under a tower of rich whipped cream as you warm by the wood stove? What's not to love about hiking in the Alps?

Now there'd be huts involved instead of tents and real food instead of freeze-dried stuff reconstituted by heating water on a tiny, unpredictable stove perched on a rock after a long, tiring day of hiking. In light of this new plan, suddenly, my wife wanted to join me, feeling "called to a sabbatical" herself.

"Of course, I want you to come!" I said. And I did. Mostly. But in my deepest heart, one of the things that drew me to this endeavor initially was solitude, away from talking, away from people, just tramping through God's high mountains, enjoying beauty, praying, journaling, and not talking as day turned to dusk, which turned to nights of shooting stars punctuating the blackened sky. Now things would be different. Suddenly, instead of forty pounds on my back, I'd be carrying twenty. Instead of the wildness of the high Sierras and

Cascades, populated by wolves, bears, and mountains lions, I'd be hiking the high Alps, populated by the constant sightings of Italians, Germans, Croatians, and Austrians. Most significantly, instead of hiking alone, I'd be hiking with someone— my wife of so many years. It's only right that she join me, because if the truth be told, she's the reason I love the mountains.

The Blonde

When I changed my major from architecture to music, I changed schools too and ended up in Seattle. That's where I met Donna, a spunky blonde who'd received a boxload of frozen king crab legs from a Coast Guard guy stationed in Alaska. He was trying to win her over with fish. Instead, after the speech class we shared, she flashed that melting smile of hers one day and said, "Do you know anyone who likes Alaskan king crab, because I've got a few dozen legs that need to be eaten, and I don't like 'em very much." I told her not to tell anyone about them, but that I, as a favor, would help her out by eating a few each day until they ran out. Her dorm room, for Alaskan king crab and tea after speech class. That's how the romance started.

The blonde's next move, though she'd never call it that, was to invite me up into the high country of the Cascade Mountains, because that's where she had what she called "classes." Their names were "hiking and snowshoeing," "mountaineering," "sailing and canoeing." With her and her outdoor friends, I, a music composition major, experienced many firsts: slept in a tent in a snowstorm on Mt. Rainier, sat down on a snowy mountain and slid out of control into a hole, learned that this snowsliding, called glissading, is more fun than walking, and stood on the starboard side of a big sailboat in Elliot Bay overlooking downtown Seattle for a rare sighting of Orca whales breaking water fifty meters from our boat. For a while, I couldn't decide if I (a) liked this girl, or (b) liked the places she was taking me. In the end it was (c) both a and b, and we were married just under a year after she'd shared her first portion of king crab with me.

After a momentary of hesitation, it was instantly apparent that she should come to the Alps with me. We've been trekking through life together, both literally and metaphorically, in excess of three decades, and she's the one who slows me down so that I can see. She's the one who aligns the countless details, so that life actually happens, rather than collapsing in on itself due to a thousand cuts of neglected "to-do's." And she's the one who makes me laugh. I've learned how to make my way in the mountains because of her. She's taught me to enjoy creation as a book through which God speaks to me in rich ways. And she's my wife, my best friend. Yes, she should come with me. And just like that, the plan mutated again. Sierra Nevada and Cascade mountains became the Alps. Solo became Duo. Plan A became Plan B.

The two of us began our quest to determine where, amidst the multiple hiking trail options in the vast Alps, we'd go. After reading about several routes, we decided to tackle a section of the Via Alpina, which its website describes as "a network of five walking trails across the eight countries of the Alpine region, more than 5,000km long and with 342 day stages." It's sort of like a "best of the Alps" compilation, offering a full variety of food and culture, easy hiking and hard, high summits, and civilized river valleys.

I'd have only a little over one-tenth of the requisite 342 days needed to complete the Alpina, so we settled, after substantial research, on a forty-day section of trail that would begin in Italy and head north through Austria all the way to Germany, and then west, ultimately curving south a bit, and then southwest, so that we'd finish in Switzerland. If all went according to plan, we'd cover about six hundred kilometers in the course of our forty days, which would mean an average of fifteen kilometers per day, about ten miles, gaining about one hundred thousand feet of elevation along the way, and losing roughly the same.

August 3. *We're in the Italian Alps, the Dolomites, hiking with our oldest daughter, since she has some time off from her teaching job in Germany, and her husband's away at training. My wife and daughter are ahead of me on the trail, and this section, after lunch, is where the real work of ascent begins. The two of them find a cadence faster than mine, and in the step-by-step rhythm of the steep ascent, I descend into a stream of thoughts about how I've ended up in these Alps at the age of fifty-eight, because the truth of the matter is that I'm not a traveler in the classic sense. While they converse, I'm alone in my thoughts. "How have I come to love mountains so much?"*

My First Love

Vacations as a child were never more than two hundred miles from home, and always two weeks. The first week was nestled in the coastal redwoods where my dad's mom was the baker at a camp for families, a camp called Mount Hermon. Salty fog hung thick in the mornings, offering a heavenly cool contrast with the oven-like heat of the flat central valley that was home. Afterward, we'd drive down the coast, stopping sometimes at famous tourist spots like Cannery Row or Hearst Castle, always ending up in San Luis Obispo, a glorious little college town near the Pacific Ocean where my mom's sister worked as head nurse at the central hospital. I'd eventually study architecture there in college.

Both places offered escape from the heat, but there was no doubt in my mind, even when I was eight, which place I preferred. As soon as we'd dropped our bags and gotten hugs and cinnamon rolls from Grandma D, I'd be off to the creek that sliced trough the valley floor of the redwood forest maybe two hundred yards away from our cabin and not more than a foot deep in any spot. Sandcastles, skipping rocks on the water, running across the suspension bridge, feet in the water. Adventure! Freedom! Beauty! Though I didn't know it at the time, the smell of the coastal redwoods would forever be linked to safety, nurture, and—though I won't try to define the word right here—holiness. Those coastal redwoods were, in every sense of the word, "mountains" for me as a nine-year-old, because, in contrast to the flat valley of my upbringing, you could hike down to the creek valley, up to the ridge, and from the beach at sunset watch the coast range turn an array of colors. And the trees, ever-green, year-round lush life. That place was like one of Tolkien's "healing houses," the place where I'd find joy and restoration as a child.

> *We're out of the valley now, beyond the initial trail that was as wide as a road and clogged with tourists hauling fancy cameras and picnic baskets because they'll walk no more than a kilometer or two before returning to their car or motel. We're also escaping the heavier air as our ascent pushes us up and over the headwall of a valley into the cool of the high country. As we ascend, I catch a whiff of pine and maybe manzanita, and this smell awakens more memories as I ascend, still mostly alone, nearing the top of the headwall, from where I'm hoping we'll be able to see the hut.*

This is the smell of my only high mountain memories from my childhood, and they're good ones too. Every summer beginning when I was thirteen, my dad would make his annual trek from our hot and smoggy valley up to little "Camp Sugar Pine" to drop me off for a week of Bible-based adventures. It got so I could predict the route, because that's what Dad, our driver, taught us to do: "Oakhurst comes first, where we'll stop for Root Beer floats; then it's Bass Lake; and after that there are exactly thirty-three turns until our exit road to camp." We'd count them out loud, my friends and I, and at turn thirty-three, Dad would angle the station wagon to the right, slip onto a dirt road for a mile or two, and then step out into another world. He'd always go straight to the water fountain, gulping a long draught and saying, "Best water in the world, Son . . . Here, try it!" And so began the annual experience at camp, no doubt the best week of any year until my dad died when I was seventeen.

In the valley, summers were so hot we stayed indoors, but TV was boring. The mountains and camp offered air that felt as if God left the refrigerator door open so you needed your sweater, and it ended up smelling like campfire smoke so that later in the heat of the valley's autumn, you could inhale your sweater and be ushered back to beauty. God also provided, in those mountains, a pond to jump in to and infinitely starry nights that made you think about eternity. The valley air back home was a smoggy cocktail of pesticides and exhaust. The mountains carried nothing save the scent of pine and manzanita (just like Italy), intoxicating for all its freedom, beauty, adventure, joy, even peace. It was in those mountains, with that glorious mountain scent as life's perfume, that I held a girl's hand for the first time, made some commitments to seek God, and later in college, prayed alone in the snow as a major step in finding healing after the loss of my dad. Mountains had become my place of adventure, beauty, healing, and most important of all, life-changing encounter with the divine.

Perhaps the most famous saying from the great naturalist John Muir is, "The mountains are calling, and I must go." This had become the way of it in my life, I realized, as I thought about what to do with the precious gift of three months off. My early experiences in the mountains gave them a reputation as a place of safety mostly, and beauty too. Since those early days, I've climbed up them, skied down them, and hiked through them. They've become a truer sanctuary for me than any church building. My theology teaches me that God is always with us, everywhere. But my experience teaches me that wild places in nature, created by God, have become places where I've been more attuned to God's Presence, where I've heard God speak. It's happened in snowy fields on starry nights; in fire lookout towers on high peaks while the sun dipped into the Pacific Ocean and painted the sky a riot of colors, in campfire circles with a single candle hanging from an ice-axe as various people tossed together by a shared hike unpeel their lives and find a vulnerability in the context of raw beauty that is, perhaps, harder to find in our safe and civilized constructs.

Hearing the mountains call to me became a reality because of misty giant Redwoods, cocoa and campfires, hugs and cinnamon rolls, and of course, the girl with the Alaskan king crab legs. We are, it turns out, profoundly shaped by our stories. Yes, the mountains are calling. I must go.

One website intended to help pastors plan a sabbatical says that a sabbatical offers the pastor three things:

- A time for personal relaxation
- A time to pursue personal interests
- A time of renewal around things that will directly benefit the congregation

It didn't take me long to determine the journey through the mountains would be the centerpiece of my sabbatical experience because mountains have been the context of spiritual encounter, healing, joy, and beauty during my entire life. That my wife shares this love of the mountains and would be joining me was an extra bonus.

"Relaxation?" Check.

"Pursuit of personal interests?" Double check.

"Things that will directly benefit the congregation?"

Hmmm. This could take a while.

Notes

[1]Stories of our Alps adventures are supplemented in each chapter with links to pictures corresponding to the stories. For this chapter: http://bit.ly /Decisions2.

[2]www.torchbearers.org is a ministry that invites people to discover the incredible reality that Christ desires to so live in union with each person that the joy, peace, hope, mercy, justice, and hospitality of Christ become real in each of our lives and pour into this broken and beautiful world through us.

SECTION TWO

PREPARING

GETTING OFF OUR BUTTS AND OUT OF OUR HEADS

CHAPTER THREE

Whatever your hand finds to do, do it with all your might.

—Ecclesiastes 9:10

*Grace is given not to them that speak their faith,
but to those who live their faith.*

—St. Gregory the Theologian

Most people I'd known who had taken a sabbatical from a life in the church centered their experience on study. They'd gone to Oxford or Cambridge to study history, theology, maybe philosophy. They'd gone to Iona to study Celtic Christianity. They'd gone to Phoenix University to get a computer tech degree so they could afford their kid's visit to the dentist. Whatever they'd done, it was usually related to study, with maybe some travel and sleep thrown in.[1]

My choice to spend forty days hiking was not just a *yes* to hiking. It was a decisive *no* to living inside my head. It was *no* to being locked away somewhere poring over books and manuscripts. It was *no* to sitting around with other pastors talking about emotionally healthy churches, or servant leadership, or why Neo-Calvinism is either vital or destructive, depending on which book I read or conference I attend. The thought of doing any of those things wasn't just uninteresting, it was repulsive. I'd sooner skip sabbatical altogether than infuse three months of my life with "God talk," or theological studies, or worse, leadership conferences. I'm not just weary of my work. I'm weary of words, ideas, and in-house doctrinal wars that polarize people who, according to the Founder of their movement, are called to unity as a major marker of their credibility.[2] I'm weary of living inside my head.

Before I proceed, maybe I should ask forgiveness. Knowing that we live in a knowledge-saturated culture, my rant might be offensive to some. Why would someone who writes books, reads copiously for both work and pleasure, and speaks at conferences react so violently to the thought of three months centered on reading, words, and study?

40

The answer has to do with a view of wisdom that stands in distinction to what often passes for wisdom in a twenty-first-century information society. Jesus, the wisest of them all, addressed this when speaking to the religious leaders of his day—the guys who made a living studying their texts, memorizing them, defending them, interpreting them, teaching them, and holding other people accountable to live by them. His assessment of these textual experts was that they "study the Scriptures diligently because [they] think that in them [they] have eternal life" (John 5:39 NIV). The observation, at first blush, seems entirely commendable. What's not to love about a group of people who study timeless truth in hopes of knowing exactly, in every single situation, how to live? Throughout modern history, it has seemed axiomatic that troubles stem from ignorance. If we only knew the right things to do, all would be well because, of course, we'd align our lives with truth, making ethical course corrections because of new knowledge and revelation. Right?

Can you hear me laughing? I just put down an article about the most recent banking scandal, whereby regulators were warned by their superiors to "overlook" violations when they involved private banks with the wealthiest clients. Marriages implode in spite of the fact that we know we're called to intimacy, and that intimacy requires honesty, vulnerability, and forgiveness. We know it's wrong to live in fear, yet we're afraid. We know it's right to live in generosity, and yet we close our fists around our assets, even as refugees, the homeless, and the abandoned continue to grow as increasingly larger segments of our world. We fear the future, fear that if we don't look out for ourselves, nobody else will. This leads us to amass vast storehouses of wealth while the vulnerable among us are left wanting. Peace eludes us, and so does justice. Why, in spite of our vast knowledge base, are we such a collective disaster?

Knowing is never enough. That's why.[3] This is a fundamental theme in all the great religions of the world, but nowhere is it more clearly spelled out than in the New Testament. We've already seen one of Jesus's statements regarding this. Elsewhere he says, stressing the necessity of serving one another, "If you know these things, blessed are you if you do them."[4] One of Jesus's most devoted followers would later say that the life of wisdom is not about words, but power,[5] and by this he didn't mean political or military power, but the power of a life united with Christ, so that divine wisdom, love, mercy, and joy might pour out from us into the real world of pain and loneliness, of addiction and fear, of violence and greed. Knowing words and ideas apparently is not enough.

Lovers of words and ideas are prone to endless study, research, and dialogue, so much so that we mistake these things for actually living. Eminem's song "The Monster" offers a chilling description of what it's like to be stuck living inside one's head, with words and ideas swirling endlessly. He talks about how hard it is to sleep when ideas start knocking inside his head in the middle of the night. We don't need to be obsessive-compulsive to know that in our information age, some of us are prone to endless research anytime we sense a change in our body. We hit the Internet in search of diagnosis and treatment. We do the same with investments, or how to treat our crying infant, or what theological nuance will lead to enlightenment. Read. Study. Research. Repeat. Are we any wiser for all of it? I doubt it. What does happen, though, is that we fall prey to the age-old mistake of thinking that because we have studied, we're better people, when in reality it's possible that all we've gained is a dose of arrogance. So thank you very much, but I'd rather walk away from words for a while. I'd rather get out of my head and into my body. Here's what happens when I shut my books . . .

August 8. It's the day of the seven summits, 15km of distance and 4,500 feet of elevation gain. We set out early, per the instructions of our hut hosts, in order to avoid potentially deadly afternoon thunderstorms. This will be a glorious day for people who enjoy the challenge of high rocky ridges, summit crosses, and exposure, but less enjoyable for people energized by safe paths through green enchanted forests.

Donna and I are the last to depart from the hut for whatever reason, and our hosts reminded us, once again, to "make haste" due to the risk of afternoon thunderstorms. I like haste, like ridges, like the adrenaline rush that comes during those sections when every step is a matter of life and death. My wife, though, doesn't share my joy here, and so the going is slow, painfully so on this very "type-A" day, slow enough that I'm biting my tongue often as I wait up ahead. Still, we're not the slowest ones on the mountain, as we soon catch up to two young German girls we'd met yesterday on the hike in. They're seventeen, out on their first adventure, and in over their heads. Denim pants. Limited route-finding skills. One of them is even wearing the wrong size boots because last night someone mistook her boots as their own in the shoe-room. They're determined, surely, but they're novice hikers on a route for seasoned mountaineers.

We'll need to pass them, of course, but instead, my wife's maternal instincts kick in, and in spite of her own fears, Donna rises to the occasion and shepherds (yes, that's a thing we pastors are supposed to do) these young ladies through the literal ups and downs, ladders and cables, terrifying heights, and slippery snow, all the way to our next destination. I'm not fuming inside, but I'm not patient either, not happy about this, especially early on when the threat of thunderstorms (which never materialized) was still a possibility. Outwardly, I'm cheering the girls on. Inwardly, I'm saying, "Why are we waiting for them? Can't they go faster? Can't you, dear wife, go faster? If we're still up here when lightning strikes and I die, I'll never forgive you." To say there's a gap between my exterior smile and my interior frustration would be an understatement. They are delightful girls, but really, it's every person for themselves when there's a thunderstorm involved, right?

Two Journals—Hers and His

Later that week, Donna will express frustration because, though she's keeping a journal faithfully, she's not feeling that her entries have any profound insights. Mostly, she's writing about the beauty of what she's seen, her delight in the people she's met, and the goodness of the food. My journal muses on racism, the culture of conformity that prevails in Austria in distinction to the bold individualism in America's society (along with assets and liabilities of each view), how especially beautiful places in the Alps are similar to some of C. S. Lewis's musings in *Surprised by Joy* and Dietrich Bonhoeffer's religion-less Christianity. My words are "deep," "educated." But they're not life-giving to me because, though I deeply love God and desperately want to discover that walking with God isn't the ridiculous burden or fool's errand so many have been led to believe, I have a tendency to think things *to death,* and when the thinking is over the joy's gone.

As my sabbatical begins unfolding, I encounter my drivenness, my impatience with people ill-prepared, my envy of those better prepared, and my inability to cherish present moments on the trail due to my eagerness to find out what's around the corner. I ask myself a question: "Is the life of faith a genuine joy for me, a reality, or is it just words?" These past years, I've sometimes felt that I'm better at talking and writing about life than living it. The temptation to equate articulation of an ideal with enjoyment of its reality is genuine, a seductive backwater for those of us living in an information age. This is especially true among the fervently religious, for whom eloquence in presentation seems enough to validate one's spiritual stature in the eyes of others.

Donna's comment about her journal, coupled with our day spent with these two German women, explains precisely why I needed to do something nonacademic for my sabbatical. The real proving ground of our wisdom and of the quality of life we're living isn't our ability to write about it or talk about it. It's how we treat people, how we live fully present in each moment by enjoying the gifts around us and seeking to serve. The truth is that my wife shepherded two women who were afraid to go on, while I, left to my own devices, would have passed them with a "be warm and be filled"[6] platitude of well-wishing. Her writings revealed a delight in what's actually happening, what she's tasting and touching. Her life on the trail revealed simplicity, gratitude, joy, a heart of compassion, and a desire to serve those in need. I was envious.

She seemed to be more fully living the life I was more skilled to talk about. Over the course of our forty days in the Alps, I would spend many moments pondering how it is that this disconnect between preaching and living had taken root in my life and others', too, these past years. One author writes that we've too often elevated the pieces of our faith that require nothing more than intellectual assent (such as the divinity of Christ, the virgin birth, the resurrection) while overlooking, or explaining away, vast parts that call us to live differently (such as the calls to simplicity, love of enemies, crossing social divides, not seeking status or power, caring for the earth).

I've lived parts of my life under the illusion that I can study life in Christ, preach and teach about life in Christ, and lead people to life in Christ simply through words and ideas. Ultimately, though, Jesus reminds us that the real proving ground of our faith isn't how articulate we are, or how profound or deep, it's how we live. I want to learn how to live a fuller life in Christ on this sabbatical, so instead of reading about faith, I'm walking through the mountains to learn how to learn what it means to *literally* walk with God.

Wilderness Walks

It appears that God teaches lots of people about faithfulness by inviting them to go on a long walk in the wilderness. Abraham walked from his previous land to his new one, then down to Egypt, then back to the new one again, and then up onto the top of a mountain for a profound encounter with God.[7] Moses walked about in the wilderness for forty years with God and spent forty intense days with God on a mountaintop. Elijah? He fought for God on a mountaintop and then ran a marathon to a cave. Jesus walked with his disciples up to the summit of a mountain, and it was there they saw a glorious future. That same future was revealed to the prophet Isaiah once, and in his writings we're told that at the end of the story all the nations will finally melt down their weapons of war and torture and oppression because peace and justice will reign. In that day, we're told, the mountain of God will be exalted above all other mountains,[8] and the nations who were previously at war will join hands and ascend this mountain together to learn the ways of peace and justice. Yes, mountains and walking are, without a doubt, a place of encounter with God.

A clear corollary to all these mountain vignettes in the Bible: being in the mountains requires walking. Step by step. All the time. We'd spend our days walking, not sitting, and this movement would become the most important piece of our experience. We'd walk when we wanted to and when we didn't. We'd walk when we were energized and refreshed and when we were tired and didn't want to go on. We'd walk in humid heat, driving rain, howling wind, wet snow, and gloriously crisp autumn sunshine. Step by step we'd walk, and it would be the actual walking that would transform us, literally, body, soul, and spirit, as I write about it in these chapters. Why is literal walking so valuable? Part of the answer is found in its power to reveal our hidden stuff . . .

February 2014. Mountains east of Seattle. *It's a training walk, a little cross-country ski outing in the mountains east of Seattle, during a week of holiday the winter prior to our big walking journey through the Alps. I have a map with the lines of color-coded ski trails on them. It looks easy enough for a guy who jogs twice a week and is decent at downhill skiing. I begin late in the afternoon, entering the forest and heading uphill, while exactly everyone else is coming down and heading out. The muted light of late afternoon, the mounds of snow clinging to trees, the silence—this is the restorative beauty of the mountains. "Forty days!" I think to myself, pondering my upcoming sabbatical. "Forty days of beauty, silence, alpine air, and the exhilaration of travel by foot." I'm gliding in the perfect snow, gradually uphill for more than a mile before turning off the outer path and choosing a different one, a path to a place called hidden valley.*

Quickly, the steepness increases, and I, the pastor who uses words about holiness and right living every Sunday, the pastor who is so very careful about the use of language, is now using "less holy words" because every step forward, I slide back, losing all but inches of my effort. I don't know how to do this sport, but I presume that alpine skiing and walking, two things I do well, have prepared me for it. I'm wrong. Halfway up this trail, I encounter a black sign with the words "Most Difficult" under the logo. The grade steepens still more, and I remove the skis entirely, now marching up the snow, gasping for air and stopping twice in the short span of this "Most Difficult" trail. Thoughts of holiness are quickly evaporating, carried away in the mist of my frosty, labored breathing.

It's then that my Achilles tendon begins bothering me. I'd injured myself the previous summer on a run (because I thought buying a certain brand of shoe would make me as fit as my favorite mountain trail runner). I'd rested it, iced it, stretched it, strengthened, and quit running. I'd presumed it was healed. But now, on this steep terrain that approximates many of our upcoming days in the Alps, the pain returns. I remember sitting at the table the night before, looking at the maps of the Alps and calculating the total mileage and elevation gain for our planned trip. I could close my eyes and easily envision our transformed bodies, strong and flexible, glowing with health because we've conquered the Alps. The trails' descriptions sound marvelous. Everything's lining up nicely. "Forty days of this!" It never entered my mind that all those uphill meters might hurt, or that my Achilles might not be able to take it. Only now am I starting to look at this through a real lens.

The rest of the journey that afternoon is filled with aches, pains, shortness of breath, some tumbles. A sudden weather change chills my core so that, by the time I return to the car, I mutter, "Forty days of this!" once again; same words, but with a different meaning than the first time we discussed it over hot drinks by the fire. For visionaries, it seems everything looks amazing until you actually begin doing it.

As long as I only read guidebooks and maps, I never for even a moment doubted my ability to pull off an epic hike through the Alps. After all, I love mountains and get inspired by the thought of doing something challenging, something epic. But inspiration evaporates like raindrops on hot pavement as soon as I face real challenges. What's more, from my chair in the living room, I can easily explain what others who've tried to make the trip and failed should have done better. Lots of us do this on Sundays. It's called "watching football," or if you're in my line of work, "preaching."

This is why so many of us get stuck. Move out of your comfort zone and you might get wet, or dirty, or break something. Get in the game and you might pay some sort of price, might even fail. Start caring for people and you'll weep, and you'll know days when you're bone-weary, precisely because you did the right thing. Better to lock the doors, surround ourselves with people who think like we do, and watch the world go by.

There's a major mindset at the core of this problem: *We've stopped living because we've come to value vicarious experiences more than real ones.* Consumer cultures offer a wide array of events and experiences for us to attend and watch for the price of admission. Sports fans in America are offered an annual rhythm corresponding to the seasons. It's winter? The Super Bowl happens, and after that there's college basketball, opening of baseball season, pro basketball and hockey playoffs, soccer and more baseball, and then the opening of football, followed by the World Series, and then, presto! It's football playoffs all over again. Another year gone by, watching rather than being on the field, talking about giving rather than giving, talking about hospitality rather than opening our homes, debating policies about justice rather than letting the realities of poverty and human trafficking push me into the arena.

I need to walk in order to discover the points of dissonance between what I say I believe and the way I live. I need to walk because I live inside my head too much, occupying a virtual world where I'm in danger of confusing who I really am with the avatar that I've become online. I need to discover how the real world of sweat and pain, heat and cold, hunger and fullness, points to the realities of the faith I study, write about, and proclaim so often. And if it's not related at all, if there's no place in my faith for pain and sweat, for doubt and discouragement, for beauty and explosive joy, I need to know that too, and change professions. I need a season with fewer words, a season where I'm just walking with God in the wilderness and letting the beauty and terror, cold and heat, rain and parched thirst, solitude and community, mold and teach me.

Time to get ready and pack.

Notes

[1] Pictures for this chapter: http://bit.ly/Outofourheads3

[2] Jesus prayed for the unity of the church and explicitly told his followers that it would be their demonstrable love for one another that would give credence to their witness. With the number of denominations ranging from 217 to 33,000+ (depending on how they're defined), it's clear we're missing the mark of unity.

[3] A second matter has to do with whether we even have the right interpretation of the matter at hand. Scriptures have been used to justify genocide, nationalism, capitalism, democracy, socialism, and both separation and uniting of church and state. I'll address this problem later in the book.

[4] John 13:17 ESV.

[5] 1 Cor. 4:20.

[6] Jas 2:16. This, too, is the point of the famous Good Samaritan story, where Jesus exposes the religious experts as educated but not transformed.

[7] The Bible is filled with profound encounters occurring between God and humanity in the context of the wilderness, and I'm presently writing a forty-day devotional about those encounters. Check the website www .stepbystepjourney.com for more details.

[8] Isa. 2:2.

EQUIPMENT

There are some secrets you will never learn, there are some joys you will never feel, there are heart thrills you can never experience, till you leave the world, your recognized world, and plunge into the vast unknown.

—Mary Schaffer Warren

It is preoccupation with possession, more than anything else, that prevents men from living freely and nobly.

—Bertrand Russell

Deciding what to carry—and what to leave behind—is always the first step.

—Belden Lane

An entire culture in America is dedicated to traveling through the wilderness with as light a load as possible. People utterly committed to this are so obsessive that they'll cut the handle off their tooth-brushes in order spare themselves the burden of that extra weight. A few training trips carrying our packs through parks in Seattle revealed the wisdom of this approach. Donna and I would come home from a five-mile walk through the park with our backs and legs a bit sore, drenched in sweat. Meanwhile, many of my training hours were spent running, and the contrast between running with no pack and walk-ing/hiking with a load on my back was an enormous chasm, like the difference between driving a car and pushing it. These experiences convinced me of one thing: I wanted as little weight as possible.[1]

Weight and Possessions

The challenge, of course, is the same in trekking as in life. One never knows what one will encounter along the way, and so the minimal-ist mantra must be balanced by attempts at assessing what the future will hold. We knew we'd be hiking at elevations between one thou-sand and nine thousand feet in August and early September, and we knew that this meant the likelihood of all kinds of weather, from sti-fling heat and humidity to rain, snow, and harsh winds. We knew, too, that we'd be carrying every extra ounce hundreds of miles, with tens of thousands of feet of elevation gain, and that even the smallest extra weight would add up to a lot of extra work.

These two knowings exist in tension with each other, each truth appealing for different choices. Listen to the weather fears and you'll pack for any contingency but work too hard. Listen to the minimalists and you'll go light but pay the price in a storm. We tried to strike a balance between the two, but I failed and paid a price. Based on the only English-language book we could find about hiking the Via Alpina, we ended up with a packing list (see appendix) and began accumulating. The centerpiece of the lightweight doctrine is the clothing—hi-tech fabric that wicks sweat away from your body so that you stay as dry as possible. You'll want a long-sleeve version, a short-sleeve version, and pants.

August 3. Sesto, Italy. *The planning and preparation are finished! We get off the bus near the visitor center in this bustling tourist town, gateway to the Dolomites, and make our way inside to confirm that the path we're about to take is, indeed, the right one. "Yes," we're told as the woman points across the street, and just like that, we begin. Lao Tzu said, "The journey of a thousand miles begins with a single step," and we begin with an adrenaline rush of excitement on this warm, sunny day, when all our dreaming, planning, and praying become reality.*

It's hot at first, down in the valley, but the going is easy. I feel strong, healthy, prepared. We're together, chatting about the stunning beauty, about the great gift of being able to be here, about how similar this geography is to our mountains back home east of Seattle. I have a watch that tells me how far we've gone, and I mark the first kilometer with my own private celebration. "Now we're getting somewhere," I say to myself, marveling at how light my pack feels, how easy the rhythm of the hiking is, how I could do this forever.

That lasts about thirty minutes. I learn quickly that the effects of everything while trekking are cumulative. Yes, the pack is light, in the cool of the presunrise morning when I've had a good night's sleep at a hotel the night before and have eaten a full American breakfast of bacon, eggs, toast, cereal, coffee, and juice. But as the day wears on and becomes hotter, and I become weary, and the full feeling that comes with breakfast evaporates, the pack magically becomes weightier, even as I lighten it by drinking water and eating food. This is a mystery I will ponder for four hundred kilometers.

By the fifth kilometer, we've turned a corner and the rocky reaches of the Italian Dolomites have come into view. They're glorious, inviting us higher, even as the cumulative effects of carrying the weight of a pack on my back step by step begin to take their toll. My back begins to hurt, and I fiddle with my pack straps a bit, because the wonderful people who made and marketed my pack had attached a little two-inch square piece of card stock which told me it's design was so amazing that I'd hardly know I was wearing it. No matter how much I tinker, though, I still know.

Having failed at finding the perfect strap adjustments, I turn in silence to a pondering of what's inside the pack. What might I shed in order to lighten the load? Other than the handle of my toothbrush, I can't think of anything.

Who carries the right amount of stuff through life? The answer, if we're honest, is none of us. We load our lives down with possessions purchased due to fear, or to fill a gaping void in our souls, or because we've been taught how important it is to match our lifestyle with those of our peers, or because we've been taught that shopping is a patriotic necessity. The fruit of this materialism, so ubiquitous in American and European culture as to be unrecognizable to us until we leave it, is that many of us are working long hours, sacrificing our health and relationships, in order to fund a lifestyle that's unnecessary and unsustainable economically and environmentally, not to mention emotionally and spiritually. Our packs are too full, and we're weary and don't even know it, because overloaded is the new normal. We'll learn on this trip how little we actually need in order to live lives rich with contentment and beauty, how rich we can be while possessing nearly nothing.

How do we put the right amount of stuff in our packs for the journey that is our lives? This isn't some sort of academic question. This has to do with how much stuff we need to live the life of fullness and joy, peace and meaning, for which we're created. How we answer the question will determine what we'll do with the rest of our days, whether we'll live lives of radical simplicity and generosity or simply allow ourselves to be swept out to sea by the powerful riptide of consumerism, even though we who claim to follow Christ give lip-service to simplicity and generosity. Words and token gestures toward justice and charity are fashionable in America, but at some level tantamount to cutting the handle off my toothbrush and giving it to "the poor." Can lessons learned by carrying everything on one's back lead to a change in some commitments both materially and socially/professionally when I return home? How much of what I'm carrying on a daily basis is because of my lust for security, approval, and significance? If nothing else happened on this trek, just finding answers to these questions would make it worthwhile.

I'm not alone, of course. Our western civilization is filled with high achievers who carry so many obligations and worries that they wear both busyness and sleeplessness as badges of honor. Robert Stickgold, one of America's leading authorities on sleep, writes that our pathetic sleep habits, born from over-stimulation and hyperactivity, are one of the chief factors contributing to diabetes and obesity epidemics.[2] Sleep loss, though, is just a presenting symptom of a deeper problem—our seeming inability to know when to say "enough." Enough money. Enough work. Enough sex. Enough social obligations. Enough influence.

Our inability here is born, I believe, from a profound sense of emptiness and a fear of the future. When hiking in the wilderness near home, I sometimes wonder if I'll have enough water and, if I'm not sure, then I fill all my water containers to overflowing at the site of the good stuff. It's a heavy load (water is weighty). Because of this, there's a sort of disappointment that sets in when, a mile down the road, I encounter a stream of pure water not seen on the map. "Had I known," I think to myself, "I'd have traveled lighter."

Millions say precisely this at the end of their lives, as they consider what really matters, and the abundance, even superabundance, they've enjoyed. While they were busy cramming their lives with more material stuff, significant relationships withered on the vine. They were busy, surely; and many were prosperous too. But what a load! Too many pay for their stuff with the precious capital of health, family, and emotional stability. As a result, we're a country filled with people who are both isolated and running on Empty because our packs are crammed full due to insecurity.

Fear of Emptiness

My adult life, through one lens, could be seen as a massive accumulation of stuff. None of us set out to make "being a good consumer" the goal of our lives. Yet over time, especially for the unexamined life, it's easy for acquisition and the obligations that go with it to consume us. A car payment here, a cruise there, a cable upgrade, and now that we have it, a bigger "smart TV" (an oxymoron if ever I've heard one), eating out more because we're too busy and tired to cook our own. Soon, our stuff defines us. It does so by demanding more time to care for it and more money to pay for it, which often means more work too. And then we're there—overworked, losing sleep, anxious, and too lonely. At the root, though, it's not just a love of new things; it's a FOMO, a fear of missing out—socially, materially, in the present, in the future.

This empty-cup syndrome is as prevalent in churches as outside them, sometimes even more so because we layer an entire level of religious obligation on top of our already full lives as American consumers. The layer we've added isn't just some sort of encouragement for people to gather on Sundays. It's much larger and carries the weight and guilt of a fabricated exhortation to holiness. Too often, we who lead faith communities have called people to get busy "working for Jesus" in all manner of activities, ranging from going overseas to hosting dinner parties, from serving on boards to taking or teaching classes. "There's oh, so much to learn, say, do, and avoid, if we're going to find ourselves on God's good side", becomes the bait, and too many people, hungry for God's approval, bite.

I'm all for serving, giving, learning, and more. Unless these things spring from the right source, however, they'll put us on a treadmill of activity marked alternatively by either pride (when we seem to be keeping all the balls in the air) or shame (when we crash and burn, as happens so very often among faithful "church people"). When this is heaped on top of the cultural expectations of upward mobility, life is often summarized by the faithful as simply . . . "busy."

The fact that busyness has now become a badge of honor is an indictment of our culture, exposing our endless lust for more. Those of us who lead big nonprofit organizations should pay particular attention, because we run the risk of playing the God-card in people's lives, motivating them to activity and getting them stuck on the treadmill, with the result that good things become burdens added to the already existing burdens of our worries about keeping up and health care, about retirement and paying for college. Wow! No wonder we're weary.

Too Much or Not Enough

On the other hand, I'll learn by experience that some careless packing and a romantic notion of being as minimalist as possible would leave me fearing for my health and safety . . .

August 13. Karwendel Alps. *This morning we will be hiking up to Bins Alm, and the weather is not cooperating. Back in the heat of Seattle when we were preparing for this trip, we'd pored over minimalist backpacking websites and determined that instead of rain parkas, we'd buy rain ponchos to keep us dry and warm during those rare times when it might rain in the Alps during August and early September. There were two problems with this plan. (1) Though the ponchos would ostensibly keep us dry, they never promised to keep us warm. Their light weight was due to their thin material, great for repelling water, but terrible at retaining body heat. (2) My poncho didn't keep me dry.*

I've had a hard time wearing it correctly, and the result is that on this cold, rainy day when wind makes the water nearly horizontal at times, droplets of water find their way into the so-called "hood," with the result that my "shell layer," intended to keep me dry, is soaked with cold rainwater. I've added to my troubles because in my romantic commitment to minimalism, said shell layer is a lightweight garment never intended to be anything other than what hikers and athletes call a base layer. On a cold, dry day, this wouldn't keep me warm. Today? I'm quickly suffering the early effects of hypothermia.

Donna, having dressed and packed properly, is enjoying the ascent from the valley to the high country. She's all smiles, stopping to absorb views, take pictures, and fully embrace the memories we're creating. Ever the one to notice the nuances of creation, she savors each step as the rare treat it is. Not me! I'm on the go, trying through locomotion to create body warmth, but failing. By the time we reach Bins Alm,

I'm in the early stages of hypothermia and recognizing that there are dangers of too little, just as there are of too much.

This too makes me think of the world we live in, a world where so many are lacking access to the basics of clean water, safe shelter, adequate food, health care, or education. We're living in a time when there are more human slaves than ever before in history,[3] a time when poverty remains entrenched across most of the globe, a time when many are trying to make it through life's journey with packs that are spectacularly underresourced for the basic journey of daily existence.

Poverty, though, isn't the sole purview of the developing world and the inner city. In our own ways, we in the West are also drastically lacking in many of the things that matter. Mother Teresa is famously remembered for observing that the deepest poverty she'd ever seen anywhere in the world was found in the United States. It wasn't material poverty, though that's present and real for many. It was relational. Millions, through disintegration of the social fabric that holds many simpler cultures together, are alone. They're alone with their diseases, alone in their aging, alone in the raising of their families due to hyper-mobility and isolation, and alone in their dying. This is a big deal for many reasons, not the least of which is that we're made for relationships. Loneliness, it turns out, is dangerous, as seen in a recent *New York Times* article: "Researchers have found mounting evidence linking loneliness to physical illness and to functional and cognitive decline. As a predictor of early death, loneliness eclipses obesity."[4]

So it turns out that, just like my packing for the Alps, I'm over-packed with nonessentials like material possessions, meaningless obligations, trivial entertainment, and a packed schedule due to fear of missing out. I'm underresourced in many of the things that matter, like sleep, eating whole food peacefully in the presence of people

I love, time to draw on the nourishment of Christ's Presence that comes through prayer and enjoyment of God's creation, and real acts of hospitality and service that are filled with delight and the capacity to be fully present.

Thoughts of "the load" that is my life will occupy my mind and heart for many kilometers in the days ahead. This is because Jesus said that if we carry the pack he has uniquely created for us, by making his priorities ours and by rooting our priorities in companionship with him, then we'll find "rest for [our] souls" and a "burden [that] is light."[5] I pack my world with stuff, and social events, and self-improvement plans, and recreation, and entertainment. The result of it all is that I feel weighed down too much of the time. I ponder why it's this way. Over and over again the words of Jesus saying, "Come to me and I will give you rest," pierce my heart. I'm invited, not to a life of mindless acquisition, not to the endless pursuit of more, even if the more is more of good things. I'm called, instead, to a life yoked with Christ, the One who walked everywhere, who had no place to lay his head, who taught people to cast aside their anxieties and live like birds and flowers, depending on creation for daily provision—without fear.

I've become convinced that to live this way requires Christ. I may have the luxury of choosing to "simplify" my lifestyle, or "go minimalist," but knowing what to keep and what to shed won't be found in a particular Bible verse. Some are called to wealth, large estates, and immense hospitality. Some are called to tiny houses. Each must find the path Christ has for us, and that's why we need not a list of which possessions are enough, but Christ as our teacher.

To be clear, I don't need Christ as a concept, or a religious guru, or the champion for my political party or narrow doctrinal fort that I protect by vilifying those who disagree with me, but Christ as an intimate Friend. It is this Friend who invites me to walk with him through daily experiences, aligning my priorities with his, my responses with his, my desires with his. Christ will call me to embrace possessions or shed them, to keep money, invest it, or give it away. To listen to Christ and follow, I'm told, will result in "rest for my soul." If companionship with Christ is a goal, then walking for hundreds of kilometers while pondering the beauty of creation should hopefully be a context in which companionship can grow, rest can be redis-covered, and we can move toward the life of peace and joy for which we're all created to enjoy.

Notes

[1] Photos for this chapter: http://bit.ly/Equip4

[2] You can read the whole story in: John Ratey and Richard Manning, *Go Wild: Free Your Body and Mind from the Afflictions of Civilization* (New York: Little, Brown and Company, 2014), 130.

[3] Jonathan Power, "More Slaves Now than at Any Other Time in History," *The Star*, October 23, 2012, http://www.thestar.com/opinion/editorialopinion /2012/10/23/more_slaves_now_than_at_any_other_time_in_history.html.

[4] Katie Hafner, "Researchers Confront an Epidemic of Loneliness," *The New York Times*, September 5, 2016, http://www.nytimes.com/2016/09/06/health /lonliness-aging-health-effects.html?_r=0.

[5] Matt. 11:29–30.

MAPS

Consulting maps can diminish the wanderlust that they awaken, as the act of looking at them can replace the act of travel.
—Judith Schalansky

There are map people whose joy is to lavish more attention on the sheets of colored paper than on the colored land rolling by. . . . It is not so with me.
—John Steinbeck

[Abraham] went out, not knowing where he was going.
—Hebrews 11:8

July 25. Salzburg, Austria.[1] *Our friend Gertraud drives us into "the city" where we'll have lunch together before catching the train to Schladming, where I'll be teaching for a few days before our trek begins. Gertraud is a longtime family friend. When my wife and I ran an outdoor program in Washington State years ago, she was our first student, coming to the States to experience the wildness of our mountains. I've often visited her and the small family farm high in the Alps, where she grew up with hard work, bitter cold, and stunning alpine beauty. One of her sisters runs the farm now, while Gertraud moved to Salzburg to become a schoolteacher.*

Maps are sold in bookshops in Europe, so we find one close to the train station with an entire wall devoted to maps of the Alps. You can buy them with less detail (1:50,000) or more detail (1:25,000). You can buy them waterproof and tear resistant, or plain paper. There are entire walls in bookshops devoted to maps. This means lots of choices, and the reality that there are two major map companies and that each company's maps have different boundaries only adds to the complexity. Add our lack of skills with German, and map shopping would be impossible without Gertraud. It takes a village to get the Dahlstroms started on their trip.

Donna has a tiny map of the Via Alpina trails, with our planned route marked out. Gertraud works with the map specialist in the book shop, and Donna and I watch as the two of them speak, Gertraud asking a question and map lady responding with the enthusiasm of rapid German and sweeping hand gestures. Though we didn't know the language well enough to understand much, we know this much: this woman loves maps! Soon we purchase seven of them, which will see us through most of our planned journey.

Whether we're navigating in Manhattan traffic or searching the first time for a trail heading in a Montana glacier park, all of us know how much visitors depend on a good map. Trails in the Alps are usually (though not always) marked clearly. At critical junctures, there will most often be a sign with either a trail number on it or the name of a destination, often with a predicated length of time added so you'll have an idea of how long or difficult the journey is. In addition, where there's a side road or a side trail along the way, there will often be a marker, just past the junction, on either a tree or a rock. It will be a swath of paint indicating that, yes, this is still the trail. These assurances are priceless when you're walking alone in a foreign country between the vital shelter of the huts, without a tent.[2]

This is all well and good, but only if you have a map and know how to read it. Without the map, the information you have in the real world lacks any reference points to put the moment into a larger context. *"Yes, I know we're here. But where is 'here?'"* is what we're asking when there's no map. In the Alps, we used every map fully, checking it so often that the cheaper maps wore through at the seams. It quickly became both a morning and evening ritual to look at the map, both to see the progress we'd made and to anticipate what was coming next. This ritual would, over time, come to have a profound effect on how I, as a pastor, view Bible study, Bible reading, and the teaching/preaching of the Bible.

Using the map in the evening as a reference point to view where we'd been was both valuable and enjoyable, because now there were experiences attached to those seemingly meaningless lines on paper. The map shows a series of switchbacks. Only afterward did we know that this section was so steep for this early juncture in our trip that we'd need to stop near the top of it for lunch because we were utterly spent. Only afterward did we know that one particular summit was flat enough for a picnic with thirty people, while another was a pinpoint where no more than two could stand without someone falling to their death. Only afterward could we identify that forest as magical, this canyon as the place where you need to wear your rain gear because the trail will soak you with snow melt, and it's unavoidable.

We thought we knew the map until we took the journey, but afterward we saw that all we knew was an approximation. Maps showed us, sometimes, that there'd be cables in this certain section of trail to aid us lest we fall. We'd arrive and discover the trail was so wide and easy that they shouldn't have bothered. Other times there was no protection. A single misstep and we'd have found the quick way to the bottom. "Would have been nice to know how narrow the trail would be here," we'd say to ourselves, a bit frustrated. We learned, in other words, that the map is not the journey. It was a paper representation of the journey, but nothing more.

Map Obsessed

As I ponder this, I realize that many religious people I know seem obsessed with the map. Defending its trustworthiness, debating which versions of the map are best, meeting in homes to study the map, writing books about the map and how to know the map. Some people are so devoted to map study they have no time left for the actual journey. These spiritual cartographers content themselves with knowledge of the land, or so they think. In reality, they're missing the point.

August 3 (evening). Dreizinnenhütte. *We arrive at our first hut in the late afternoon. As soon as we're above the head-wall of the valley, we hear dozens of bells ringing, echoing off the carbonate rock walls that give these southern Alps their own distinctive beauty. The Dreizinnenhütte is perched on a ridge overlooking "The Three Sisters," a stunning uprising of three rock faces that draw climbers from all over the world. We check in, pouring the possessions of our pack onto our cots in "the lager," a giant co-ed dorm of just over a dozen cots. I remove my hiking shirt, drenched in sweat, and put on my other shirt, a dry long-sleeve affair, along with a light-weight jacket, and we all make our way downstairs to the dining area.*

Knowing that in just a couple hours we'll eat a large meal with all the other folks spending the night in the hut, we each opt for a light snack and gaze out the window at the ever-shrinking visibility. The sisters who were on display in all their glory an hour ago are hidden now, shrouded in a coat of fog, as if modesty suddenly became fashionable. We eat, rest, and then make our way down to the common room for our first big meal in a hut.

The entire evening is utterly other than any analogous experience in my life. Seated with strangers from different parts of the world, the feast of the night isn't just food, it's conversation—the shared bond of being mountain lovers overcoming language and cultural differences to create mar-velous connections and conversations. When we can eat no more, dessert comes, and when we can eat no more again, I see that things have cleared outside, that the sisters are out for sunset.

I excuse myself from the table before the others leave and embark on what will become a familiar ritual: Go upstairs and acquire warm clothes. Go to the shoe room and shed hut slippers in exchange for hiking boots (which are strictly forbidden in huts, for reasons having to do with the cow pastures through which all hikers have walked), and head outside. Only now can I see the other side of the ridge on which the hut is perched. The rocky landscape slopes gently downward for about two hundred yards before dropping off utterly, forming the vertical headwall of a different valley with its own stream that will feed the river.

The sun is setting, turning the clouds to the west a fiery and ever-darkening orange, even as the mountains become all shades of blue, fading to black. It's quiet, and if you listen hard enough, you can hear the stream, three thousand feet below. Shafts of light sever the sky, and it looks as if God is speaking, only it's not metaphor. God is speaking, at least to me.

It's the first night of our trek, and I feel a strange cocktail of excitement for the days ahead, coupled with bone-weariness from the preparation to get here and the twenty years of work leading to this break. All of it settles in just now as night is poured into the sky, conquering daylight slowly but inexorably. The colors keep changing, subtly, but endlessly, as if the palette is infinite, until there's nothing left but the dark beauty of mountain silhouettes. And silence.

I breathe deeply—deeper, it feels, than I have in twenty years—as I'm finally pausing long enough to reflect, receive. There's an emotion beyond words as I look, alone, at the beauty before me. This art, this doxology of holy elegance, happens millions of times a day in the heavens and on the earth, and who's paying attention? I sit, and something wells up deep within me, an emotion or state of being I've not known for a long time. I'm near tears as I offer thanks for various gifts and listen for the voice of Christ.

"Thanks for the light show," I overflow.

"I am light, and what you see is a tiny taste of the beauty that is my light. I long to shine into the darkness of poverty, addiction, rage, violence, isolation, greed. Let me be pure light to you, Rich. Let me pierce your heart with beauty. Come on, man. What's holding you back?"

Tears rise, but I don't know what to do with them, don't know how to answer, so I keep praying. "Thanks for the waters down there in the valley."

"If anyone's thirsty, let him come to me and drink. People don't need religious obligations and fear-based ethical constructs. They need the water of life. Drink from me, Rich, always, before anything else. Come on, man. What's holding you back?"

It goes on like this for a few more minutes, the Spirit of God present in a tangible way. Maybe God's voice is always present that way, but it gets overwhelmed and interrupted by traffic noise and commutes, virtual relationships, the sales register, and the chatter of shame, lust, comparison, and the insecurities echoing inside our heads. I believe all of us have a longing for God's perfect peace,[3] God's shalom, residing deep in our hearts, so that in this moment when I experience a taste of it, I'm undone with joy and healing. I hear more from God as stars appear, as I listen to One I've loved for years but who often withers in significance because of the religious icon I and all the other spiritual professionals so very often turn him into, reducing this flaming love and glory to words and programs.

I realize here in this darkness, with the sound of the stream's headwaters below, that I want the light of Christ; I realize that pockets of darkness remain in me in spite of (maybe because of?) my religious professionalism. I pray that the light will shine freely, unbound by darkness.

And I'm thirsty too—thirsty to know my neighbors rather than being so drained after work that all I can do is watch stuff on my device, thirsty for an environment where grace is real enough that people can live authentically and know they'll still be loved, thirsty for margins wide enough to pay attention and care for the people I work with. I'm thirsty for slow, for joy, for peace, for strength—I, the one who knows, loves, and preaches about Christ am thirsty for Christ. I stay and pray until there's nothing left to see. I'm changed, having met Christ in his creation.

These moments at the mouth of the canyon were some of the most beautiful and powerful I'd ever experienced, melting me with the fire of God's love and shattering my defenses with the piercing beauty of God's invitation to jump fully into the infinity that is God's majesty, beauty, and grace. I'm forever changed because of what happened in that intersection of space and time.

Of course, it would have been just as effective had I stayed home and read the map, or watched something on PBS about the Dolomites, right? That's the danger in a culture that values education more than experience, ideas and the virtual more than concrete realities, maps more than travel. Increasingly, we've come to equate virtual relationships with relationships, vicarious experiences with actual experiences, and intellectual ascent of certain truths with knowing in real experience the truth that, alone, sets people free.

In his classic TED Talk, "The Demise of Guys,"[4] Phillip Zimbardo articulates the challenges men face with the overwhelmingly easy access they are granted to virtual relationships, particularly porn (which kills the capacity for intimacy and social skills), video games (which kill social skills and foster passivity and consumerism), and fantasy sports leagues (which create physical passivity and sluggishness of both mind and body). The challenge, at every turn, is that our culture is offering vicarious substitutes for reality. Why is this?

The foundational problem isn't video games. The problem goes all the way back to Eden, because it was there that our true nature became embedded in our hearts. It was there, in the midst of perfection, that a wrong choice was made. This was followed immediately by another stunningly wrong choice. When God began looking for Adam in the garden, Adam said, "I heard the sound of You in the garden, and I was afraid because I was naked; so I hid myself."[5]

Naked encounter is what we fear most of all—with God surely, but, as the story unfolds, we see clearly enough that our fear of vulnerability and exposure extends to one another as well. We fear being known, believing the lie that to be known is to be judged, to be unworthy, and hence to be isolated. We deal with these fears by preemptively isolating ourselves, and we have been at it long before video games and porn offered cheap and easy escapes from the terrors of reality.

Map Faith

The most deceptive forms of isolating, though, aren't KKK robes, but respectable religion that deftly substitutes debate and doctrine for relationship and grace. It's nothing new, friends. Jesus spoke to the religious leaders of his day and told them that they, in essence, were far too in love with the map. "You search the Scriptures because you think that in them you have eternal life," Jesus said to a crowd that contained some religious textual experts who were offended by his recent healing of a man on the Sabbath because healing on the Sabbath was like coloring outside the lines—unacceptable to the religious elite whose major concern was conformity.

So here's Jesus appearing to commend his detractors by telling them they search the Scriptures. Who wouldn't think highly of searching the Scriptures? We teach our children to search the Scriptures. We hold games and contests motivating them to memorize the Scriptures. I preach from them every single Sunday, and lots of people come to listen! We debate their meaning and seek to be known as "people of the book" because we believe God has spoken. Yes, it seems searching the Scriptures is always and only a good thing.

Except . . . no. Jesus goes on to say that they search them because of their (mistaken) notion that in them they have eternal life. But the Book and the words of the Book don't bring life. Christ brings life, not words about Christ. The distinction seems unimportant to some—nothing more than semantic word splitting. "Of course, Christ is life, but he's not known without words," they say. That isn't the issue though. Jesus is trying to show highly educated and deeply devoted people how easy it is to substitute knowing and defending words about Jesus for the reality of knowing him. It's tantamount to favoring the map instead of the journey, like believing that vicarious living and intellectual assent constitute spiritual reality. When this perspective gets too deeply embedded, bad things happen every time, on both personal and collective levels.

On the personal level, "map faith" causes me to profoundly miss the point. Called to a journey that will make me look more and more like Jesus over time, I instead end up not just slipping into failure once in a while, but actually harboring huge swaths of character deficiency, perhaps without even knowing it. That's why, on the whole, church people look so very similar to the surrounding culture. They embrace the same consumerism (and bankruptcies), the same self-medication habits (and thus addictions to porn, alcohol, and more), the same idolatry of individualism (and thus the same isolation and relationship failures). The fact that the deeply religious sections of America also have the highest rates of teenage unwed pregnancies should, at the least, cause us to ask why there's a strong dissonance between what a faith proclaims as its ideals and the practices of its adherents.[6] "Map faith" allows me to miss the mark because my calling and commitment to look like Jesus has mutated and become instead a commitment to believing things about Jesus.

A quick view of church history shows us that many cultures have missed the mark here, including our own. Christianity has been wed with colonialism, land theft, genocide, slavery, sexual abuse, and environmental destruction, all carried out by and amongst people gathering weekly to worship the Prince of Peace who loves the whole of humanity, who calls us all to freedom, simplicity, and contentment. This contradiction is inevitable whenever the map becomes more important than the journey.

Twenty-first-century faith is at risk of yet again creating a host of casualties due to "map faith." We argue about the map: Is it inspired, inerrant, authoritative, or all three? Is it perfectly accurate or just accurate? Who made the map? Humans, or the Holy Spirit, or both? Which translation of the map is most accurate? Are lesser translations safe for travel?

We teach about the map, describing the journeys of others in detail and sharing about how marvelous it is to take the journey ourselves. "Yes," we think to ourselves. "Marvelous." We sing songs praising the map and listen to sermons rearticulating the words of the map. Unless we take the journey, though, this map-worship becomes, ultimately, boring and meaningless.

The point of having a map is so we're empowered to take a journey that will transform us; any lesser use for the map misses the point. We must—must—take real steps toward becoming wholly holy, in real life, with our money, our bodies, our time, the freedom with which we share our stuff, and how we relate to people different than us, if we're going to know the real beauty of Jesus. Studying and defending the map will never be enough.

If I'm going to be out there for forty days, I need to get in shape. But it turns out that the real "getting in shape" would happen once we started our journey.

Notes

[1] Photos for this chapter: http://bit.ly/Themaps5.

[2] Traveling without a tent, unthinkable in North America in most hiking situations, is the norm in Europe because of the culture of huts, about which I'll write in Chapter Eleven.

[3] Volumes have been written elsewhere about the Hebrew word *shalom*, which is decidedly more than merely the absence of conflict, though it includes that. *Shalom* has to do with everything being made right; relationships reconciled, bodies healed, union with God restored, justice prevailing, forgiveness poured in. We taste it occasionally, and when we do, this sense that "we're made for this" is what we feel and experience.

[4] Phillip Zimbardo, "The Demise of Guys," YouTube, September 24, 2001, https://youtu.be/oVEHeY8sY5Q.

[5] Gen. 3:10.

[6] Tanya Lewis, "Teen Pregnancy Rates by State," *Live Science*, May 5, 2014, http://www.livescience.com/45355-teen-pregnancy-rates-by-state.html.

SECTION THREE

JOURNEY

ADAPTATION

Life requires of man spiritual elasticity, so that he may temper his efforts to the chances that are offered.
—Viktor E. Frankl

All we have to do is decide what to do with the time that is given to us.
—Gandalf

So choose life in order that you may live.
—Deuteronomy 30:19

AD-AP-TA-TION: a change or the process of change by which an organism or species becomes better suited to its environment.[1]

As a result of rising every day, hoisting a pack on our backs, and walking for four to ten hours, we changed. Our bodies changed. Our perspectives on the world changed. Our sleeping and eating patterns changed. Most significantly, our capacity to handle stress changed, for the better. Though we still had the same names, jobs, passports, and marriage papers that were ours when we arrived in Europe, the truth of the matter is that we'd head back to America different people—body, soul, and spirit. Our transformation came about because of two things: the environment we chose to place ourselves in, and our response to that environment.

This observation is so self-evident that it hardly seems worth mentioning, let alone devoting a chapter to unpacking. Of course, we're changed by our environment. We're blank slates "written upon by experiences," as B. F. Skinner implied so long ago with his behaviorist approach to psychology. Skinner would go on to boldly declare that people "have no free will—a person's environment determines their behavior." This has become axiomatic enough in some circles that people absolve themselves from responsibility for their actions by claiming it was family issues, skin color, or an economic condition that determined their choices and situations. We don't act on the world. The world acts on us. It's a clean and easy way of looking at the world. Cause and effect. Closed system. Modern. Sane. Predictable. Done.

If only it were true, we could move on. But it's not. Skinner largely presumed (at least in his popular representations) that our environments are dictated to us. Although this is often true, the reality is that many of us have the freedom to create our own environments. We make choices about where to live, whom to marry, or whether to marry, and what to do with our resources of time and money. Will we go hiking this weekend, or watch TV? Dance, or watch football? For most people who are reading a book like this, the majority of our environments are of our own choosing. I choose this academic major, these friends, this fast food, those responses to betrayal, this spouse. I choose work over family, or vice versa.

There are exceptions, of course. We don't choose our family of origin and the many consequences that flow from that. We don't choose whether we have better skills in music or basketball, or whether we grow up in mountains, valleys, or near the ocean. We don't choose the faith environment of our childhood. Poverty or wealth, developed or developing world, black or white—these realities and many like them loom large in shaping my values in life, and they're not to be taken lightly.

They are, though, not the whole of the story. Many of our environments are born of our own choices.

What Is My Basis for Choosing My Environments?

This journey taught me that the there are two larger "environmental" questions that will determine the quality of my life.

September 4. Brand, Austria. *We load our packs for a day hike to the top of Mottakopf. The hike ascends three thousand feet in three miles, a rapid enough ascent for a real challenge. Most of the time we're above treeline, meaning the path's exposed, dropping away steeply and seemingly endlessly, so that falling is not an option. The exposure awakens my senses, and I'm mindful of the vital importance of each step.*

As the steepness and exposure increase, the trail diminishes to nearly nothing, and it starts to rain. Donna, never a fan of steep drops, views the rain as a sign that she's had enough and declares she'll wait for me. We're only a few hundred vertical feet from the top by this point, so I quickly press on.

The wind increases with every step as I approach the exposed ridge. Within ten minutes of leaving Donna, the cross marking the summit is in sight. I make my way toward the ridge and am hit with the full force of incoming winds. Clouds are racing across the sky in some sort of frenzied churning, as if late for a party. Mountains vanish under their cloak and then reappear again, and I laugh, mindful of the pure joy I feel in the moment. There are disappearing acts everywhere. Each time a mountain becomes visible again, it's in different light and somehow more beautiful than just seconds before.

I walk into the wind toward the cross that marks the summit and suddenly find myself on top of the world, alone, in Austria. I take a picture at the cross and am hit with an overwhelming wave of gratitude—for this joy, this moment, this body, which this past winter was fighting me with an Achilles injury. But here, now, we've been trekking daily for well over a month, and our bodies are strong and fit, maybe more than they've ever been. They've adapted to the environment we gave them.

Donna writes in her journal from that day, "On the way back down, we saw beautiful older couples out for walks in their beloved mountains. I want to grow old well. I need to maintain this level of activity. . . ." Later that evening, we'll dine in Brand, chatting with a couple we'd met earlier in one *of the huts. Our bodies, souls, spirits seem to be whole in this moment, and we're enjoying a taste of what can only be described a shalom!*[2] *All is well.*

"*I need to maintain this level of activity,*" is an important phrase that will determine a major change in our lives when we return to normal life. This is because there's a strong weight in our culture lulling us to choose inactivity over movement, insulation over weather, sitting over just about anything else. Living in our climate-controlled spaces with access to virtually everything without ever needing to get out of bed, we frankly have little need ever to move our bodies or to be outside. Cars, stairs, elevators, desks, fast food, easy chairs, beds, done. A default position of inactivity prevails in our modern world, and though rest is important, it's only real rest when it functions as a counterbalance to activity. Take away the activity and rest becomes sloth.

The Rewards of Sloth

"Sloth nation" might be an overstatement, but not by much, as evidenced by the continued rise in rates of obesity, diabetes, and heart disease. There's even more to the story, though, as recent discoveries in the medical world seemingly confirm what many ancient cultures knew all along: each of us is an ecosystem of body, soul, and spirit. Neglect any single part and the whole will suffer. John J. Ratey, MD, has served up a feast of new discoveries linking our minds with our bodies. In *Spark* he writes:

> At every level, from the microcellular to the psychological,
> exercise not only wards off the ill effects of chronic stress;
> it can also reverse them. Studies show that if researchers
> exercise rats that have been chronically stressed, that activity

makes the hippocampus grow back to its preshriveled state. The mechanisms by which exercise changes how we think and feel are so much more effective than donuts, medicines, and wine. When you say you feel less stressed out after you go for a swim, or even a fast walk, you *are*.[3]

Each of us is his or her own little ecosystem, and what we do with our bodies will have an effect on the whole of us, soul and spirit as well. If you don't believe me, just ask the students of Naperville who began a program called "zero hour PE" before their academic classes. Students in the program used heart monitors and were graded on how much time they spent in their various aerobic zones. In 1999, students participating in this program placed first in the world in a global science test, and sixth in math. But more than academics are at stake here. Dr. Ratey goes on to cite the ever-mounting evidence linking our lack of exercise with a host of problems, including anxiety disorders, ADHD, depression, and addiction.[4]

I knew that choosing movement would make my body stronger. I didn't know how profoundly it would affect my soul, my spirit, my wholeness, and my joy. It makes sense, though. When the Scriptures tell us that we're "fearfully and wonderfully made," the "we" in that declaration is referring to our whole person. What's more, we're made for a purpose, and that purpose will find expression in and through our bodies, so we'd be wise to take care of them as the gifts from God that they are. One of the wonders of our body is how, when we choose the right amount of movement, it feeds our souls and spirits, fostering the wholeness and joy for which we're created. This is because we are, if not "born to run," at the very least, "made to move."

I spoke with two Italian brothers who'd been trekking together in the Dolomites every summer since they were teenagers. They're in their late seventies now and still going strong. They had all the elements of what I call "thriving"—broad smiles, ready laughter, strong handshakes. We were standing just outside the door and people were loading their packs for the day and moving on. One them approached and asked me if I'd be willing to take their picture. He handed me his camera and they stood in front of me, vibrant, with arms thrown over each other's shoulders and eyes that looked eager for the day ahead. They'd be putting in 20km, they told me, and I said, "I want to be like you when I'm older. How is it you're still out here enjoying all this?"

The older one spoke. "We decided a long time ago that if we ever chose to stop moving, it wouldn't be long before 'not moving' would be chosen for us. Years ago we committed to doing this every summer, and because we do it every summer, we keep moving in the winter too so that we're ready."

A Moving Environment

Choosing an environment of movement for my sabbatical was one of the best decisions I ever made, because the aftereffect has been a new lifestyle of movement. We learned through our days in the mountains that our bodies crave activity. We've been rewarded with greater measures of whole health—body, soul, and spirit.

There's more, though. I learned from the experience of choosing movement that nearly every choice I face deals in either life or death. Life-giving choices happen when I move toward the life for which I'm created, toward my deepest and truest identity. This principle goes all the way back to words spoken by Moses, who spoke on behalf of God one day on a mountain. After laying out for the future a set of values that will lead to life and offering warnings about the consequences that will come should we abandon those values, Moses speaks: "I have set before you life and death, the blessing and the curse. So choose life in order that you may live, you and your descendants."[5]

Choose, in other words, what leads to wholeness, fullness, joy. We'll make a thousand choices every day:

- Take the stairs or the elevator?
- Make eye contact or stare at the floor?

- Encourage or be cynical?
- Eat chicken nuggets coated in chemicals and fried in bad fat or eat real food?
- Speak or be silent?
- Forgive or get bitter?
- Squander our precious moments staring at pixels on a screen or jump into face-to-face, flesh-and-blood reality?

Music choices, sexual choices, time-use choices, buying choices, giving choices—all of these are in front of us every day and moving us toward either life or death.

Choosing life doesn't usually mean choosing the path of least resistance. God knows there were days in the huts when it would have been easier to choose staying in bed late and adding extra whipped cream to a second serving of strudel. Choosing life, though, means choosing that which will feed life, and these choices are often an act of faith, because we live in a world where choosing destructively is often our default. Faith believes, though, that there's a payoff in choosing generosity, hope, forgiveness, truth telling, whole foods, contentment, movement, enough sleep, and, oh, so much more. We won't choose perfectly, but our confidence in the long-term value of choosing life will give us the courage to follow the hard road more consistently. Therein we find adventure, transformation, and joy!

It's tempting to think that our lives are formed in the big moments and big decisions, but the reality is that our lives are formed step by step. Back when newspapers existed, I'd rise early, bring the paper into the house, and put the rubber band binding the paper on my rubber band ball. I'd been building the ball for years to remind me that no single rubber band seems significant. It's the day after day seemingly meaningless additions that have the cumulative effect of making something big, something visible, something with bounce.

Our days consist of a thousand tiny choices: Being fully present with someone when they're speaking. Seeing someone in need and offering timely words of encouragement and affirmation. Cooking real food, exercising, praying —none of them headline-making. You're doing them precisely because you know they are character-making, and that's what matters most.

How Will I Choose to Respond to Imposed Environments?

During our forty-day trek, it rained about two-thirds of the time. Locals called it "the summer that wasn't," telling us that this happens about once every ten years, and that we're "just lucky" to be here for this one. Nobody prefers trekking in rain over sun, but along with us, thousands of hikers in the Alps are still at it in weather "not of their choosing." We're all pressing on by adapting, internally and externally.

Layering

I've written elsewhere about how important it is to have various layers of clothing that we can wear and shed throughout the day depending on the situation. Base-layer, mid-weight layer, and shell create a sort of trinitarian essence for hikers. Layers are then added and removed depending on the situation to adapt to whatever heat, cold, wind, rain, sun, snow, or sweat that come our way moment by moment. With this threefold layering approach, you have everything you need for almost any situation. Having them, though, and using them properly are two different matters.

Knowing the right resources to draw upon in the various situations is called wisdom. Ecclesiastes 3 tells us that there's a time for everything. But knowing what time it is? That's the challenge we all face. As I walk the Alps on a morning of constant weather changes and adaptation, I ponder the link between adaptation and sustainability in other areas of life, like marriage, faith, and vocation. I think back to moments with my children when I should have offered comfort but offered correction instead. (My son broke his elbow once while running on the pavement, and when he came screaming in pain, I lectured him about the dangers of running on pavement, even as he wept in pain. "Correction first, comfort later," a response countered by my wife, with the result that I discovered the person most in need of correction in the moment was me.) How many times have there been when I should have spoken, but remained silent, when I should have challenged conventional wisdom, but chose the easy path of conformity instead? Looking back, I can see that the wisdom of knowing how to adapt in various situations is critical to our well-being and wholeness—a skill that must be learned. The right layer for the right moment.

The church and her people have failed here often. We've found a layer that worked for us and clung to it even when seasons of life changed. But our clinging created blind spots, especially among religious leaders. Jesus had more trouble with that demographic than any other, because they would build systems, and then protect and defend them until they had hardened and fossilized. "This is how we wash our hands. This is how we eat our food. This is how we practice Sabbath." Over time, it got ugly in covert ways unrecognizable to the leaders: "This is how we condemn people different than us. This is how we elevate our reputation among our followers. This is how we kill Jesus in pursuit of protecting our tiny version of the truth." What they were really saying, although they didn't know it, was, "This is how we fail to adapt."

We who are "faith leaders" need to acknowledge our problems here (and the term "faith leaders" includes every person seeking to help their children, friends, neighbors, or coworkers follow the way of Christ). Not always, but too often we've chosen self-righteousness over love, violence and retaliation over peacemaking, shaming over forgiving—all the while worrying more about the kind of music in our services, or the way we do communion, than representing the character of Jesus. We have a long history of scandals—financial, sexual, and political—that have led an increasing number of people to reject any organized expressions of faith, choosing instead to self-identify as "spiritual" but "not religious." The biggest tragedy in this is that the people walking away aren't rejecting Jesus; they're rejecting the sad caricatures of Jesus we've created, the tiny ones that make Jesus look like a wealthy republican, a hip environmentalist, an angry protestor, or a paranoid cave dweller. Truth be told, the Lord of the universe can't be constrained by any of our categories. We need to adapt so that we can keep moving toward looking like the compassion, mercy, joy, hope, peace, service, and generosity that is Jesus.

The way forward isn't found through withdrawal into one's own isolated, self-made spirituality. We're better served by looking to Christ on a moment-by-moment basis for our ethic. Speak or be silent? Give or withhold? Confront or comfort? Usually the right answer is "God only knows," and the good news is that Christ will show us the way. But this requires real communion with Christ, a communion nurtured through a blend of text, creation, prayer, and community. Each layer is vital in equipping us to adapt, and those who refuse to use all the layers miss the destination of looking like Jesus.

Attitude

In addition to layering, there's an adaptation of attitude that's equally vital, especially when we find ourselves in environments we would not have chosen. The people who hike through these Alps come from many nations. The ones we met ranged in age from maybe six up through the early eighties. In spite of age, culture, and geographical differences, though, these trekkers were bound together by a sort of "can-do" attitude that was infectious.

Lizumerhütte. *Klaus is seventy and has come to the Lizumerhütte from the Glungezerhütte, which means he came from the hut to which are headed. It is a cold and* *cloudy day, perpetually threatening to storm without ever actually doing it, though a biting wind howls for the duration, stealing body heat whenever we stop moving. We are fortunate to be at the same table as Klaus for supper, and he is bursting with joy, eager to show us pictures of the day on his camera, eager to talk about the special beauty of the wind and cold, and eager to move on tomorrow to discover new beauty. He's been in the Alps for thirty days already and has two more weeks planned. His favorite word, repeated often as punctuation after describing a view for us as we huddled around his camera, is "Fantatisch!," which needs no translation. His seventy-year-old eyes speak of life, and an eagerness to make it around the bend to see what's next.*

Klaus was the rule, not the exception. Take the four men in their forties, celebrating their twentieth year trekking together. The day I met them and shared a drink, we'd all arrived by breaking a trail through a foot of snow. "We never let weather stop us," they said. "In fact, we never let anything stop us, because if we did, this commitment would have ended years ago. Instead, we know we'll do this every year, and it's deepened our friendship at a time when most men are waking up to middle-age loneliness. Whatever the weather, we're in!" We met this same attitude over and over again. People made a choice to engage together in this, and then, having made that choice, chose a positive attitude when the environment became less than ideal.

The beauty of our trekking days often had to do with the reality that they were non-negotiable environments. We'd wake in the morning at point A and begin walking to our destination at point B. Along the way, we'd encounter steep, cold, snow, rain, wind, heat. Our environment was dished up on a platter, like a diner with one item on the menu. As a result, we began to see that the most important thing was not the weather, nor the steepness of the trail, nor the humidity on warm days, nor the clarity of the trail markers on those days when markers were few and far between. What mattered most in determining the quality of the day was our response to it all. Everything started inside our heads and worked out from there. As the days turned into weeks on our trek, the realization that I'm able to choose my response to both my internal and external environments hits me like a ton of bricks, as the saying goes. I'm almost giddy with the realization that my responses aren't dictated to me by a mysterious inner force—they are *mine*, consciously chosen. I remember a moment of hunger and heat when I consciously detected frustration and complaint welling up, and instead, I willfully chose joy. "Amazing," I said to myself. "I can choose." Where had this truth been all my life?

Learning this lesson may turn out to be the most valuable thing I bring home from my sabbatical. My hope is that I'll absorb these truths of adaptation at two levels, both personally and as a leader. Adaptation is important to me personally because I'm prone to melancholy, which leads too often to choose cynicism and disengagement. I'm beginning to see that I waste too much energy mourning my circumstances, wishing they were other than they are. I'm not talking about a death in the family here. I'm talking about, "Why do I have so many appointments this week? Why can't our city leaders get their act together and make room for the growing number of cars rather than trying to make us all ride bikes? Why are people complaining about my leadership style? Why is it still raining in Seattle?"

Rather than adapting to my environment, I sometimes fall into the pit of whining, wishing the rains of my problems or pains would just go away. When I'm done, nothing is changed, of course, other than that I'm now sour on life, thinking the worst of most people around me and wanting to quit my job. I'm supposed to help people rise above their circumstances. But while trekking, I'm mindful of the times I've been stuck wallowing in mine instead.

Paul the apostle wrote a letter from a Philippian jail in which he said, "I want you to know that the things that have happened to me (arrest and imprisonment) have actually advanced the gospel."

Dietrich Bonhoeffer, himself no stranger to prison and eventually martyred for his resistance views towards Hitler's Reich, wrote, "I believe that God can and indeed intends to allow good to emerge from evil, even from the greatest evil. To that end, he needs people who make the best of everything."[6]

Roger Williams led a Christian camp and fought a battle with cancer for many years before finally losing. I asked a coworker of his what attitudes he chose, and he said,

> In the midst of cancer giving Roger a much shorter life
> than anticipated, he chose joy. He laughed, he loved, he
> worked and didn't complain. One of the greatest gifts he
> gave our staff was a relentless commitment to use his gift
> of encouragement to the very end. In the midst of his own
> suffering and decline, he told people how much he valued
> and loved them. His legacy included modeling joy in
> tough circumstances.

The reality is that all of us have the freedom to choose our response, to make our own weather, as one leadership guru likes to say. This, of course, is a core principle of what it means to follow Jesus too, for the Bible is filled with crossroads and choices. "Choose life," is what Moses shouts from the mountain to the millions below who are ready to begin a new chapter in a new land. The words are poignant because he knows full well that our default mode is to choose whining and naysaying, gossip and lassitude, which are all simply synonyms for choosing death. Paul told the Philippians to choose joy—consciously.

We are, all of us, prisoners of our environments at times, but we're never prisoners of our choices. Victor Frankl was a Jewish physician and therapist imprisoned in Auschwitz along with his wife. She was executed and he lived on, moving to Vienna after the war and writing *Man's Search for Meaning* as a catalog of things he learned in the prison camps. He wrote, "Everything can be taken from a man but one thing: the last of human freedoms—to choose one's attitude in any given set of circumstances, to choose one's own way." We have the freedom, in other words, to choose joy, love, service, sacrifice, compassion, no matter what is happening outwardly.

As I encounter people choosing joy in the midst of heat, rain, snow, wind, and overcrowded and stinky sleeping conditions where we're stacked together on a platform, it begins to sink in. Choose joy! Choose gratitude! Choose life!

Environment Shapers

The principle is important for any who are influencers in the lives of other people, which is basically all of us. We carry an energy that displays whether we have chosen joy or allowed ourselves to default into self-pity, cynicism, or bitterness, the common languages of our broken world and broken culture. Our private choices affect our public personas, though we wish they didn't. Addictions lead to shame. Shame leads to withdrawal. Withdrawal leads to discouragement and more addiction, and it often presents as anger. It's a vicious cycle, and countless people are caught in the crossfire of it.

We who shape the lives of others are invited to the challenge of embodying hope in the midst of the loads, disappointments, hungers, and difficulties that are our lives, and then calling others, as Paul does from jail in Rome, to "follow (our) example." Yes, we're in environments, but we are environment-makers too, and the sooner we realize that and begin choosing joy, hope, and gratitude on a consistent basis, the better. Our world thirsts for this kind of hope and joy.

I know there's a time to mourn. I know about authenticity and the folly of singing praise songs after a bomb's gone off downtown. I know about lament too, quite well. Those aren't on the table in this discussion, though. It's not joy or lament, hope or mourning. It's joy or whining, hope or cynicism. When the latter are our choices, there's only one right answer. Both Paul and Dietrich Bonhoeffer wrote from prison, and both taught us that real wisdom, real power, real wholeness don't reside in our capacity to build "the life of our choosing." Nobody is granted that privilege in any sort of unrestricted manner, because cancer happens, or infidelity, or terror, or a refugee crisis, or a cell gone wild to mar a fetus with a confining disability. Life happens.

Frankl, Bonhoeffer, and others like them, taught us that the blessed ones find ways to embody hope, serve others, and live with joy and generosity even in the unchosen circumstances that become their prison. For this to happen, they say, we'll need to be willing to fight on the most important battleground of all, over and over again—on the battleground of our mind. Paul taught us that we must take "every thought captive to the obedience of Christ."[7] This is Paul's way of saying that once we see how important our thoughts are, we'll no longer passively let them create storm clouds of anger, anxiety, regret, and so much more that will simply blow in uninvited on the winds of circumstances. Instead, linked with Christ as our companion, we will choose joy, and when we do, something profound happens. Then we'll sing with Habakkuk:

> Though the fig tree should not blossom
> And there be no fruit on the vines,
> Though the yield of the olive should fail
> And the fields produce no food,
> Though the flock should be cut off from the fold
> And there be no cattle in the stalls,
> Yet I will exult in the LORD,
> I will rejoice in the God of my salvation.
> The Lord GOD is my strength,
> And He has made my feet like hinds' feet,
> And makes me walk on my high places.
> (Hab. 3:17–19)

Do you know what I have to say about that?

    Fantastisch!

Notes

[1] Photos for this chapter: http://bit.ly/Mapjourneyadapt6.

[2] According to *Strong's Exhaustive Concordance*, *shalom* means "completeness, soundness, welfare, peace."

[3] John J. Ratey, MD, with Eric Hagerman, *Spark: The Revolutionary New Science of Exercise and the Brain* (New York City: Little, Brown and Company, 2008).

[4] Ibid.

[5] Deut. 30:19.

[6] Dietrich Bonhoeffer, *Wondrously Sheltered* (Minneapolis: Augsburg Publishing, 2006), 28.

[7] 2 Cor. 10:5.

CHANGE—WHEN GOALS GO UNMET

The real damage is done by those millions who want to "survive." The honest men who just want to be left in peace. Those who don't want their little lives disturbed by anything bigger than themselves.
—Sophie Scholl

*This time, like all times, is a very good time—
if we but know what to do with it.*
—Ralph Waldo Emerson

*Forgetting what lies behind and reaching forward
to what lies ahead, I press on toward the goal for
the prize of the upward call of God in Christ Jesus.*
—Philippians 3:13–14

Lots of wilderness literature is written by people who didn't reach their goals. He set out to hike the Appalachian Trail, and didn't finish it. She set out to hike the length of the Pacific Crest Trail, and didn't finish. They sought the summit of Everest, but there was a killer storm.[1]

August 4. Dreizinnenhütte. *We wake up to beautiful weather, and after breakfast enjoy a full day of hiking. We start by dropping down into the glorious river valley where I met God so profoundly at sunset last night. The early morning sun highlights the vast and varied wildflowers which adorn the headwall of the river valley. This slows our descent dramatically, because every corner is a new expression of beauty. We must stop, must absorb, must remember.*

Little do we know at the time that our preference for absorbing beauty over making mileage will become one of many factors that will lead us to ditch our original itinerary. As we make our way deeper into the valley, we enter shade again, as if the sun's going down at 9 A.M. Soon the sun breaks over the ridge and its warmth blankets us. Then the valley drops in elevation, and we're back in the cool shade. Sunrise over the ridge. Shade. Sun. Shade. "Sunrise. Sunset. Repeat." All the way down the river valley.

By late morning, we're down from the high country. In the heat of the valley, we shed some layers, knowing that in the next hours we'll gain back again all the elevation we lost in the morning. We're quickly into a slow rhythm of ascent, steadily gaining altitude and overcoming gravity step by step. Just before heading over a pass, we stop for lunch and I unfurl a lightweight piece of foam. I've brought it just in case we're stuck between huts, so that we'll have some comfort while we sleep—under our ponchos that supposedly double as tents. It quickly becomes apparent that this will never happen, short of someone having a heart attack or a broken leg, so by the end of the tour I'll ditch this item as worthless bulk.

There are places in the Alps where trails are cut literally through the rock and the side of the mountain, sometimes creating a bit of exposure where a fall could be costly. The alpine clubs of Europe mitigate this risk by attaching cables to the rock for the hands, sometimes drilling a little rebar into the rock to assist with footing as well. Our fee for joining the Alpine Club helps fund the annual maintenance of these important safety aids, and now we're about to encounter the first of these sections.

The narrative about this section of trail says, "There is no room for vertigo here." And while that might be slightly true, we are underwhelmed by the level of exposure. The trail feels as wide as an office staircase, and the cables seem unnecessary for most of this section, which then drops into another river valley, our third of the day, before our final ascent. At the top of the headwall there's a World War I memorial, one of the common alpine reminders that we are walking not just through geography, but time. Since mid-morning, our entire path has been marked by vestiges of the war, decayed gunner stations on the side of mountains buried in trees, and what appear to be barracks. This real estate has changed nations countless times through the ages. We are presently hiking through what was once Austria and is now Italy. The result of this is a funky cultural fusion of schnapps and lasagna, schnitzel and red wine, strudel and espresso—the glorious intersection of our favorite foods, which our trekking allows us to indulge in guilt free!

From the ridge, we walk a short forty-five-minute descent to Dürrensteinhütte. By the time we get there, we're tired, having hiked all day, gaining roughly three thousand feet in elevation. We drop our packs just as rain starts spitting from the sky, and Donna goes inside to check in. She's back out quickly with sad news. "No room."

"But the book we read said there's always room mid-week."

"No room."

"But they must take us in. We're Alpine Club members."

"Yes, they'll let us stay here: On the benches in the bar. After it closes. At 10 P.M."

This is disappointing news, but thankfully they tell us there's a hotel in close proximity to this hut (the only time we'll experience this during our entire trip), so we hoist our packs again and make our way another two kilometers down the road to Hotel Geisl, which has been owned by the same Austrian family since before the war, when this little slice of Italy was Austria. Our hostess speaks better German than Italian. The food, architecture, and decor are all thoroughly Austrian, twenty-first-century evidence of the nineteenth-century Hapsburg empire's expansive reach.

After showers and an elegant meal, we decide to make reservations for the next three huts, so we call ahead. Wednesday? Full. Thursday? Full. Friday? Full. The intermediate hut that's not on the itinerary but is on the route? Full. In every case, we could technically arrive and the hut would need to shelter us, but the notion of waiting for the bar to close every night before finding a place to lay our heads isn't appealing to us, in our late fifties and wanting our beauty sleep. We sit at the table, poring over a map, with no place to go.

Soon, we'll make our way down the river valley in search of lodging while we reconsider our plans, but even in the valley, with dozens of guesthouses and hotels, we'll fail to find anywhere to lay our heads for the night. "Italy is full in August," becomes a mantra we hear enough during our search that, after a dozen failed enquiries, we believe it. "Have you tried Austria?" someone suggests. "Lots of Austrians come down here in August, so I think they might have some rooms up there." And just like that, our initial plan for the Via Alpina collapses under the weight of fully booked Italian huts.

Goals are nice, but here's a word to the wise: don't marry them. This applies not only to trekking in the wild, but also to business, money, and just about all of life. Better to let yourself be blown a bit by the wind of the Spirit, as Jesus likes to say, than reach your goal only to realize that the mountain you chose to climb wasn't actually intended for you at all.

We made a map of our planned route, and now the rest of the huts between here and the Austrian border appear to be full, so regardless of our energy, skill levels, plans, and desires for pasta and wine, we're leaving Italy. Call it poor planning if you like. I'm a bit more generous with myself and tell people that (a) there wasn't much written in English about this Via Alpina, and (b) the single book we did read was written by people who said they'd had no trouble finding rooms in the Italian huts without calling in advance, and (c) we thought our membership in the club would grant us rights, not to sleep on tables in the bar, but in real beds in real rooms.

I like reaching goals so much that when I don't reach them, I always wonder what went wrong. I'll go back over the pursuit, scrutinizing every detail to determine where I failed, or others failed, and what should have happened to change the outcome. So this turn of events was more than disappointing. There were little shaming ghosts hovering over my head whispering, "You're a terrible planner. You've ruined your wife's trip of a lifetime." It was a low point.

Within forty-eight hours of our "No Vacancy" experience at the Dürrensteinhütte, we're on a train, flying across the border at breakneck speed in contrast to the walking we've been doing, as we make our way to Innsbruck to recalibrate our trip. It won't be the last time we'll recalibrate. Within a week, we'll be sitting in Lamsenjochhütte high above tree line, trying to decide whether to proceed to Falkenhütte or bypass it by heading back down into the valley we'd just come from. I'm all for proceeding, in spite of the fact that later on this route there is a high exposed ridge with bouldering skills needed, and as such, not my wife's favorite terrain. "She's tough," I tell myself, and her. And she is.

Plans change, though, because I meet four men from Belgium, poring over their maps at the hut as they warm themselves from the storm outside with beer and pasta. They tell me that they've just come from Falkenhütte, and that with predicted heavy rains, that route will be both "brutal and risky." Being a sensitive husband, I'm weighing whether or not to share this with my wife or keep it to myself and press on, when they add, " . . . what's more, a section of the trail's turned to rubbish, and there's a detour. It'll take you several extra hours to get to the next hut."

Since the day, without the detour, is slated for 15km, sharing seems appropriate, and we decide to head back to the valley from whence we've come. This is because the itinerary is filled with 15–20km days, and the reality of such distances in the mountains is vastly different than the same mileage at home, walking around the lake by our house, which is flat, paved, sea-level, and nearly climate-controlled due to Seattle weather. We'd read about how on these 15km days, there were all these marvelous side trips that were "must see": summits to conquer, farms to visit, historical sites to discover. Our 15km days were doable surely, but with relentless altitude and weather changes, they generally took everything from us, leaving little energy or desire to see anything. Already the demands of the distance had pressed us into a pace that not only made extra sightseeing uninviting; it made even stopping to enjoy the beauty of the trail challenging.

The thought of missing the beauty because the pace dictated that we must press on felt so wrong that we finally abandoned our planned trip entirely and built a new itinerary. Yes, the remainder of the trip would still be trekking in the Alps. Yes, there'd still be a rhythm of ascent into the high country, time there, and descent again into the river valleys. No, it won't be one long line anymore, starting in Italy and ending in Switzerland. Instead, we created a series of loops in various regions of the Alps: Dolomites. Tuxor. Karwendal. Garmish. The Alps near Fusson. And finally, the Ratikon Alps, before returning to the Dachstein range in Austria. Goals? Poof! They're gone, swept away by the flood of realities ranging from overbooked Italian huts to washed out trails.

Dangerous, Disappointing Goals

Goals and plans are funny things. You're taught to be ambitious, taught that you can do anything or become anything if you're willing to work hard enough, so set some goals for yourself and go after them. There's just enough truth in the statement to make it dangerous. It's dangerous for several reasons.

First, there are limitations, as I learned in fourth grade when the music teacher looked at my mouth and told me it was no good for playing the clarinet. Or when, at sixteen, I turned out for summer basketball league just before starting high school. I worked as hard as anyone at basketball with the goal of playing high school ball. For three previous years, I had come home from school and shot baskets into the hoop my dad had ceremoniously put up when I became a teenager, saying, "This, Son, is what teenage boys do!" I'd gotten good enough to make most of my shots, even from way beyond the three-point line.

Still, I was only five feet, six inches tall and 135 pounds. My school had two thousand students, and this meant that there were lots of people taller, faster, and stronger than I was. When I'd try to shoot, it was different than at home, alone in the driveway. These taller, faster, stronger guys were in my way. They knocked me over. They stole the ball. When I tried to do the same in return, they still knocked me over. They blocked my shots and easily shot over my short head.

After I spent twenty minutes pursuing my goal, the coach called me to the sideline. "Listen, Rich," he said. "Someone told me you're good at music, that you're going to play drums in the bagpipe band. Right?"

"I'm hoping to," I replied, sweat dripping off my featherweight frame.

"That's great. I think you should stick with that," he said, and he took the ball. He subbed someone in for me, and that was that. Basketball career? Over. Desire, hard work, goals, none of them could make up for a vast height-and-skill deficiency.

All this comes back to me and has me wondering about how we deal with unmet goals in our lives. I know people who've spent their whole lives wanting to do this, but are doing that instead. You can have a goal to get married and still be single, have a goal of wealth and be stuck in poverty, have a goal of owning your own business and having that business fail in spite of your best projections and hard work. What then? Should you declare yourself a failure and just take up drinking, profligate sex, or endless TV?

Another danger that comes from setting goals is what happens to some of us after we fail to reach them. I'm now convinced that worse than missing the goal is the guilt we heap on ourselves because we tried, really went after it, and came up short. This guilt is tragic. I will contend with every fiber of my being that the reaching or not reaching of goals is, in the end, not much of a thing, because goals aren't inspired. They aren't delivered in the mail by God with a list of consequences should we fail to achieve them. We had a goal that would have pressed us into longer distances every day, and because stuff happens, we changed our plans.

Yes. We could have slept on benches. We could have travelled 15–25km every day. We could have done the trip exactly as planned. What's more, since we didn't do it as envisioned, we'll never know what kind of trip it might have been. We might have come home in such spectacular shape that we'd market our new theology of body in some sort of program to get baby boomers outdoors exercising, and made a small fortune. We might have had countless stories of the adventures we'd gained by pressing through even more fatigue and fear, of proceeding on trails that were even more dangerous, of how our amazing courage transformed us.

Or we could be dead. We'll never know, because we changed our plans. Late in our trip, Donna spent a night cataloging the trip we actually took in contrast with the one we'd planned. This was much harder for her than me, and it began a discussion about goals that would prove to be liberating and life-changing for both of us. Here's what we learned about goals: *Goals get us moving, and that's their greatest value.*

We had decided to hike the Via Alpina, and when we did the math, it turned out that it would be nearly four hundred miles in forty days. Instead, we ended up with a bit over four hundred kilometers in forty days. Is this failure? It all depends on the lens through which you look at it. If your life depended on four hundred miles, then yes, you failed. In our case, though, the goal got us into the Alps, where we stayed for forty days, adapting the scope and length of our hikes because we had other goals that were even more important than the magical four hundred miles number, namely to rest and have a challenging, life-giving, restorative time.

Many would be the day during our time that I'd look around at the stunning beauty. I'd ponder the fellowship we'd enjoyed the previous night with fellow-hikers or with the owners of tiny guests houses. I'd consider the reality that because of preparing for this trip, I'm in the best physical shape of my life. I'd think about the vast stores of health, wealth, and energy Donna and I have at our disposal, enabling us to take this trip of a lifetime. More often than not, I was overwhelmed with gratitude and joy, recognizing the countless great gifts I'd been given in my life to bring me to this point, and this realization created in me the space to pray about how I can better use everything entrusted to me as a means of blessing others in the years to come. And all this came from going after a goal I failed to reach.

So yes, I'd say unmet goals aren't necessarily indicative of failure. This is true, as well, for the countless athletes who compete but don't win. There's value in going after it, even if you never reach it, because it's the pursuit that gives structure to our lives. During our final days in Austria, we met lots of cross-country skiers who were here in order to start getting in shape for their coming season. They train by a combination of hiking in the mountains and cross-country skiing on the Dachstein glacier. We'd seen dozens of them, but, of course, only one will win the prize. And the others? They'll enjoy the blessings of travel, health, challenge, and the beauty of creation, just for starters. Losers? Hardly. They're committed, profoundly transformed by competing, whether they win or place last.

More important than reaching or not reaching our goals is the choosing of our goals. The cultures we live in saturate us with their attempts to shape our goals for us so that they can then offer us products, at a price, to help us reach them. Fix your body. Make more money. Go to school to get a better job. Find the perfect match.

Increase your market share. Save the environment. End human trafficking. Bring peace to the Middle East. Get out of debt. Lower your blood pressure. Clearly lots of goals are out there vying for our attention and investment. Which ones should we go after?

Paul the apostle offers two critical bits of wisdom about this. First, he warns us against passively allowing our goals to be shaped by what the culture tells us is important. "Don't let the world squeeze you into its mold," he says, because if you do, you'll have the same anxieties, addictions, idols, body-image problems, sexual dysfunctions, phobias, and anger problems as the rest of the world. Something will eat you up, leaving you frustrated and empty, in spite of your many pursuits.

But Paul says there is a goal worth pursuing in earnest. It's the goal of knowing and enjoying profound intimacy with Christ, because with this as a foundation, all the joy, love, mercy, wisdom, peace, strength, and power of Christ will find expression in your actual daily living. These will be born in each of us differently because they will be unique expressions of Christ in us, but they'll be born as certainly as Christ was born. This birthing, however, is the fruit of your declaring and pursuing the ambitious goal of "knowing Christ"— not as a theory or doctrine or ideology, but as your closest friend, source of life, and lover.

Some of the countless moments of silence that unfolded during our journey were spent thinking about the future. I've been at the same job for twenty years, and the work I love has grown in scope and complexity. I need to make decisions about which route to take in the future, and so should I ask myself why we choose this trail rather than that one? How often are we motivated by fear or by a lust for financial security or prominence? What should motivate us? When we're at the various major crossroads, are we reading the signs right? Sometimes it appears they're in a foreign language.

We fixate on particular decisions too much, I think. "This job or that?" "Is it time to move to a different city?" "Should I buy a big screen, or the biggest screen?" Each question is undergirded with a boatload of assumptions, a way of looking at the world. Perhaps it's those assumptions that need reordering, prior to the making of decisions.

This is why Paul declares that knowing Christ is the "mother of all other goals," the foundation from which my priorities in life should be born. I stare at a sign, written in German, which begins with "Achtung!" (attention). The good news: I know this sign is important. The bad news: I don't know enough German to read the rest of the sign. If I had the mind of a German, I'd know. But I don't. And as I stand, staring at the sign, a word from the Bible echoes around in my brain: "We have the mind of Christ." I see that my future depends on letting Christ's mind so saturate my own that I gain a different way of looking at the world, that I come to know the language of God, as it were, so that I can read the signs.

All this begins by making "knowing Christ" the starting point of my life, rather than an accessory or option. The fruit of such a union won't be religious zeal, fanatical theological flame-throwing, burnt-out leaders, or people who toss around God-words on the surface but underneath are driven by motives of pride, or greed, or insecurity. The fruit will be real love, joy, peace, compassion. The fruit will be a life that has enough bandwidth to genuinely care for people. The fruit will look like Jesus.

I know this, teach this, preach this. But my actual life reflects it only sporadically. I'll come to see that sometimes, to my horror, it's my religion that gets in the way of my faith. It would take a few experiences early in our trip to remind me that knowing Christ and finding a real union with him, more than any other goal, is what I must make my life about.

One of those early experiences would be a day of exposure.

Note

[1] Photos for this chapter: http://bit.ly/Change7.

EXPOSURE

CHAPTER EIGHT

The task must be made difficult,
for only the difficult inspires the noble-hearted.
—Søren Kierkegaard

Be careful how you walk.
—Ephesians 5:15

Follow me.
—Jesus the Christ (Matt. 4:19)

There are days in life when we're vitally aware that every step matters. There's a job interview, so she pores over her résumé, chooses her clothes and make-up carefully; even shoes are up for debate. There's a big test, a thesis defense, a first date, a decision to make an offer on a house, or to take the job or not. In these moments, we're careful how we walk because there's an existential realization that the stakes are high.[1]

August 7. Glungezerhütte. *This hut sits at twenty-six hundred meters. We arrive there feeling strong, whole. Part of the reason is because we shaved a thousand meters of our ascent off quickly and easily by riding the gondola from Innsbruck rather than hiking, thus saving time, calories, and energy expenditure dramatically. It's around 2 P.M. when we come inside, out of a biting wind, to the warmth of a fire, the smell of pasta, and light jazz wafting through the speakers of this quintessential Austrian hut.*

After a marvelous meal of pork medallions and sauerkraut, the proprietor shares that he'll be offering a final weather update regarding tomorrow at 8:30, at which time he'll tell us whether to take the high or low trail to Lizumerhütte. Without Internet, and with only spotty phone coverage, nearly everyone up here is dependent on the nightly weather report offered by the hut host, and in this case the report will determine both the route and the time breakfast will be served. If thunderstorms are pre-dicted, breakfast time will be adjusted early enough to allow people seven full hours of hiking before the anticipated time of the storm.

The main hall is crowded at 8:30 as the report is offered by this stout man with a full gray beard and enough of a twinkle in his eye that you both know he loves his work and wonder if, when the huts close in October, he becomes Santa—the real one. The report is a full fifteen minutes, and there's uproarious laughter along the way, but it's all in German, so I sit at the edge and wait for Jonathan, the German-speaking American from Cleveland, to come trans-late for me when the meeting's over.

As people disperse, he says, "It's supposed to pour rain all night long and then clear before sunrise. Thunderstorms are anticipated tomorrow afternoon, so breakfast is at 6:30, and he says we must be on the trail by 7:30."

"High or low?" I ask.

"He says tomorrow will be an amazing day to take the high trail—views in every direction. The trail is on the ridge the whole way." I smile, nodding. I know the meaning of the words "ridge" and "trail." Little do I realize what they will mean when taken together in these Austrian Alps. I ask what else he said, because he spoke to the group for fifteen minutes. "Just jokes about Americans," he says, and we leave it at that as we start to hear the pelting rain on the roof of the hut, the sound we hear even louder an hour later as we drift off to sleep, wondering if the weather report will turn up true in the morning.

I'm up at 6, and a quick step outside reveals that we're starting our day above the clouds and will ascend from there.

Seven summits await us, as we travel along a ridge to the south and east, covering a mere 14km but taking nine hours to complete. This is because, as we'll discover later, this is an alpine route which, according to one website, "should only be attempted by those who have appropriate mountaineering skills and experience," which is, we come to find out, part of what the host said the night before in German while I was reading a book in the corner.

This isn't much of a concern for me because I have the appropriate mountaineering skills. I've climbed enough in what might be considered dangerous places to feel comfortable on exposed rock ledges and ridges. My experience has given me confidence on rock, and ironically, confidence begets a relaxed yet utterly alert and focused demeanor, which makes the exposure feel even easy by virtue of familiarity. You come to realize, after not falling time after time, that you're as likely to fall as a good driver is likely to simply veer into oncoming traffic and die in a head-on crash. Yes, it could happen, but it probably won't, so you don't worry about it. Good drivers aren't constantly thinking, "Don't drive into the ditch—avoid the ditch—watch out for the ditch." They've moved into a different zone of quiet confidence, even at seventy miles an hour. It's like that with decent rock climbers and high places.

As the day progresses, I realize quickly that although I have this assurance on exposed rock, my wife doesn't. As we ascend, a few summit crosses come into view, and we're struck with the realization that each of the summits must be obtained today. It doesn't matter how we feel about attaining them, whether excitement or dread. The path forward will be up and down, along this ridge, for the next eight miles.

This, in itself, is daunting, but the true nature of the hike doesn't reveal itself until after the first summit. Beyond the cross, there's a descent that by the standards of any hiker who doesn't climb would be harrowing. There are vertical, nearly vertical, and beyond vertical drops, at least fifteen hundred meters down, just beyond the edge of the "trail," but that's the wrong word. In fact, there is no trail, simply red and white paint on boulders, showing hikers which rocks to scramble down, but it's clear that a single misstep at the wrong place means certain death.

For those with experience, this is not intimidating. You simply don't fall. Inhale deeply, relax, and focus on each step. For those lacking experience, this is terrifying, because every step is saturated with the fear of falling—which creates anxiety, which creates muscle tension, which creates rapid weariness. My wife's in the latter category, as are the two German girls with whom we're hiking, Felicitas and Inge. They're both seventeen and are here in the Alps in search of their first grand adventure. On this day, on this ridge, they've found more than they bargained for (see Chapter Three), but they, like the rest of us, must continue.

I loved the day of seven summits. Truth be told, I find the exposure, the sense that every step matters, energizing. This is because I love activities that are so demanding that my mind is reduced to consideration of the single thing in front of me. Here's a ladder bolted to a rock face. We must descend it. On the one hand, it's a ladder. The fact that ladders have been part of our lives, that we've climbed down dozens, hundreds of ladders in our lives, means that we know this much: we can climb down this ladder. On the other hand . . .

> *. . . this ladder, suspended in space, will be completely unfor-*
> *giving should a hand or foot slip during descent. There'll be*
> *no recovery, no next steps, because wrong steps will be final*
> *steps. So, yes, though this is "just a ladder," this is an impor-*
> *tant, high stakes ladder. It requires something different than*
> *the two states of being that often are our default positions in*
> *life, for neither fear nor familiarity will be helpful. A third*
> *way is needed.*

It's here we pause to consider the two deadly poisons of fear and familiarity. They rob people of living the life for which they are created, deceiving them into settling for far less, for glittering pursuits that overpromise and underdeliver, instead of days filled with meaning, joy, purpose, and hope. We must expose them for what they are: liars and thieves that prey on our weakness to make us weaker still. There's a third way, utterly other than the paths rooted in these deceptions. It doesn't have a name but is rather the byproduct of dealing wisely with these two impostors.

Beware of Fear

In the days after my sabbatical, as I write this, the fear factor in the lives of Europeans and Americans is rising exponentially. We're afraid of shootings, of terror, of wacky politicians coming into power, or corrupt ones remaining in power. Some are afraid of immigrants. We're afraid of failure, rejection, myriad forms of illness, poverty, betrayal, loneliness, and more. Fear has become a strong enough force in our culture that people are increasingly defining success as "not failing," which means not falling victim to any of the things we're afraid might happen to us.

This is a very small way of living. It would be tantamount to defining climbing as not falling, which is absurd on two levels. The objective of climbing a rock face or a mountain is to get to the top. Calling it a "good day" because you failed to fall is essentially what more of us are doing, more often than ever before. We're defining health as avoiding illness, defining calling as being employed, defining intimacy as staying married, defining security as money in the bank. By changing the rules and lowering the bar regarding what constitutes the good life, we can feel "good" about ourselves.

Except we can't. As we watch TV or cat videos on YouTube, or fall in bed at the end of another tiring day of obligations with an early dread that tomorrow we'll need to do it all over again, there's a nagging feeling that this isn't the life we've been created for. This "don't fall" mentality infects people of faith too, with what I call a fixation on sin management. When faith is redefined as "stay sober, stay married, tithe, pay your taxes, read your Bible, and go to church," we've functionally changed the goal from reaching the summit to "not falling." It's sin management. It creates judgmentalism, pride, and hypocrisy. And worst of all: it's boring.

In contrast, God's text, offered to us to point the way toward real living, is shot through with invitations to a wholeness, joy, strength, and generosity that looks so very different from merely avoiding common notions of sin. God has a summit for us, and it looks like this:

Vitality— *"Those who wait for the Lord will gain new strength; They will mount up with wings like eagles, They will run and not get tired, They will walk and not become weary"* (Isa. 40:31). We're promised a capacity for living that's beyond the norm of just surviving. We're promised a strength not our own which will enable us to enjoy life for a long time without the prevailing weariness, boredom, fear, and cynicism setting in. This promise alone is enough to wean me off of the sin-management paradigm. But there's more.

Abundance—*"The thief comes only to steal and kill and destroy; I came that they may have life, and have it abundantly"* (John 10:10). This word "abundance" implies a capacity to bless and serve others, even in the midst of our own challenges and messes, even if, like Jesus when he was washing his disciples' feet on the night of his arrest and impending execution, we're about to die. I long for this capacity to be fully present each moment, listening, loving, serving, blessing, encouraging, challenging, healing. I'm invited—even called—upward to the high country of actively blessing my world, rather than just surviving.

Wholeness—*"[God] made Him who knew no sin to be sin on our behalf, so that we might become the righteousness of God in Him"* (2 Cor. 5:21). Yes! The invitation goes beyond "not sinning" (as we religious people typically regard not sinning). The vision is much more positive, more summit-like. God lets us know that we're invited to nothing less than displaying his character in our daily living. The good, generous, gracious, righteous, wise, loving, and holy God is inviting us to embody and enjoy these same qualities as they find expression in our own daily living. Summits. All of them; they're ours to enjoy—and, yes, getting there will require conquering fear.

Reaching any of these realities, though, requires facing down exposure, and our day of seven summits taught us that there are timeless principles for facing exposure well. They work on rock faces as well as oncology floors at the hospital, in unemployment lines, and when we're rebuilding a life after profound loss.

Face Exposure with Acceptance Rather than Judgment

After the third summit, we take a photo with our companions, the two seventeen-year-old German girls who are out in pursuit of their first adventure. We survey the descent that's yet ahead, followed by yet four more exposed ascents on rocky ridges with carefully placed cables as aids. It looks daunting, and it is. Inge speaks of the challenge ahead, how frightened she's been, and how she's not so keen on continuing, but then adds, ". . . and yet we *must* do it."

Exactly! The beauty of this particular day is that not ascending is not an option. I must proceed forward if I'm to reach the next hut, because there's no shelter between here and there. The only other option is returning to last night's hut and then hiking all the way back to Innsbruck. It's go forward or miss the whole reason we came here. No, simply not falling won't cut it on this trip. We have a place to be which requires we deal with our fear of falling. And for this, I'll be forever grateful.

Fear of falling must be overcome in real life too, lest we settle for sin management and a shallow kindness motivated by fear of rejection or conflict. We must climb the high exposed ridges of generosity, where giving is sacrificial and leads to trust. The cliffs of freedom from addiction must be scaled, and this will require the risks of vulnerability, confession, and the courage to face our pain. The steep rocks of love for the stranger and refugee are vital terrain in this age of fear, but it requires living with the realization that your open heart and home are at risk by the very nature of opening them to people you don't know.

The faith mountaineers who have gone before us have shown us the way. They opened their homes and hearts, giving freely of both time and money. They stood for the disenfranchised and oppressed, some at the cost of their lives. They risked vulnerability in their pursuit of wholeness and healing, coming clean about their addictions and infidelities. They forgave betrayals in Rwanda, England, Pennsylvania, even when it hurt to do so.[2] They rose above the valleys of mediocrity. Had their paradigm been merely "not falling," they'd have stayed home, or stayed bitter or afraid. But alas, the focus of the life we've been created for is the summit, the high calling of embodying and giving voice to hope and mercy in a despairing world. When this is the vision, the risk of falling is, by comparison, inconsequential.

How often has fear been the governing force in my life? The miles provide abundant space for contemplation of that very thing. I recall moments of disengagement from hard conversations, moments of avoiding difficult people, moments of cutting conversations short—all born of fear. In the step-by-step journey of this sabbatical, especially on days of high-ridge exposure, I'm mindful that I don't have a fear of falling off rocks; but I do have a fear of falling out of people's favor. When I was a child, my family, especially my mom, was driven too often by fear of rejection. She'd work herself sick during the holidays, making sure floors were waxed enough, pie crusts flaky enough, our Christmas tree perfect enough for the relatives who'd be coming over. These were people who lived a mile from us and who were in our house most normal days of the year, but parties required performance and exhaustion, or so it seemed. Fear of rejection stole her joy and wearied her body.

I've feared rejection more than a few times along the path that is my life, and the results haven't been pretty. Like the fear of falling, fear of rejection has paralyzed me, filling with me anxiety over the choice of my words and hyper-sensitizing me to whether or not someone was validating me. This is a terrible way for anyone to live!

So there it is. I'm afraid. Since returning from my sabbatical, there have been dozens of times when I've named my fear of an impending difficult conversation, changes in the work I lead, tough decisions, or painful realities forced on me through the health challenges of loved ones. Each time, I can hear Inge's voice: "And yet we must do it!" echoing in my soul. This is because the reality of what must be done is right here in front of me, and it's pointless to wish I were elsewhere, or that this relationship were other than it is, or that this decision had fallen to someone else. Such wishing, I've come to see, is anxiety inducing and feeds my bent toward cynicism. It is a waste of energy and a faith-killer.

Right here. Right now. This is my life. Maybe I want to ski more, and I tear my ACL. Maybe you want to stay married, but your spouse's addiction to violence is destroying any semblance of safety, let alone intimacy. Maybe you want a promotion but have just been passed over, or applied to graduate school and didn't get in. You want health, but it's cancer. Whatever your state in the moment: this is where you are! Acceptance is the starting point, because then you can focus your energy on your journey rather than on wishing you were elsewhere.

Face Exposure with Protection

I've been able to overcome the fear of falling in the high country by spending time on rocks, climbing and falling. A maturing happens in climbers' bodies as they adapt to the demands of strength and balance needed for their sport. Last summer, climbing in Austria with some friends, I was able to enjoy some highly exposed climbing where falling would have meant certain death. I got to do this precisely because I was tied in to the rope. The more I trust my protection, the less afraid I am to fall. The less afraid I am to fall, the more relaxed I am. The more relaxed I am, the better I climb.

It's precisely here that the Good News of Christ has proven to be most life-sustaining to me. For me, the appeal of Christianity has never been much about gaining a "get out of hell free" card from God, though I believe that to be both true and important good news. My story, though, of adoption and the early death of my dad, is a story of Christ answering the emptiness of my life with companionship. "Father to the fatherless" is how it's phrased in the Bible, and this has double significance for me.[3] I heard at a winter camp that Jesus is about relationship, and though I'd grown up in the church and even given lip-service to this notion, it somehow struck me with full force after the death of my dad and the gaping crevasse of loneliness that I'd fallen into. For the Jesus of my childhood, companionship was not the first, or even the second, reason Jesus came. First was dying, and second was "to show us how messed up we were so that we'd see our need."

While these two truths about Jesus, preached weekly in the church of my childhood, matter, the front door I walked through when Christ became real to me was God's invitation to companionship. Suddenly, I saw the phrases "I am with you" or "I will be with you" all over the Bible, and the delightful story of Jesus seeing a tax collector up in tree and telling him to come down because he wanted to come to the man's house for supper! The invitation to companionship was there all the time, but it was hidden because of the lens through which I'd been looking. I'd grown up trying to "get right with God," but the "I am with you" teaching became foundational for my maturing. The "with-ness" of Jesus as my companion became the source of protection that has seen me through both falls and exposed dangers during much of my adult life as a husband, father, pastor, leader, and friend.

Protection doesn't mean we're wrapped in a magic bubble and granted immunity from any suffering or loss. Such notions of faith are nonsense. They over-promise, underdeliver, and leave a host of burnt out and cynical "ex-Christians" in their wake. Real protection isn't immunity; it's the knowledge that we are never alone and will never be alone, come what may. Christ as our constant companion can never be lost, and this is enough, because Christ is the headwaters of peace, hope, mercy, and joy. "Who do I have in heaven but you, and having you, I desire nothing else on earth" is how Asaph the songwriter says it. On my best days, I believe it, and the reality of being yoked with Jesus gives me the courage to stare fear in the face and shoot for the moon instead!

Beware of Familiarity

Hidden in these narratives about fear are the dangers of fear's sister, "familiarity."

"Just like climbing a ladder," I say to myself once again I as I prepare to descend. I know this ladder, in this moment, is a big deal in my life. It's bolted to a face, having just four rungs, and descending to a small narrow ridge on which we'll continue our journey, buttressed by a cable in some places and calling for naked balance elsewhere. This continues until things widen out again, providing a moment of security and solidarity on this route of relentless exposure.

Everything around the ladder falls away into space, perhaps two thousand five hundred feet down to the bottom. Yes, it's just a ladder, except that falling off the ladder in my garage costs me six feet and maybe a bruise or sprain. Lose contact with this ladder, though, and life is over—you'll miss grandchildren and weddings, laughter and good coffee, late-night conversations and stunning sunrises. You'll miss the richness of seasons changing, or praying with friends. In short, you'll miss the glory of living with eyes wide open to the glory of God that is all around you and the Christ that is within you as companion, because you won't be alive at all. This ladder, in this moment, is suddenly everything. "Richard! Pay attention."

And so I do. Facing the rocks, my back pointed outward to open spaces of a deadly free-fall, I slide my foot down onto the ladder. I check twice and then invest my weight on the rung. It holds. I'm careful to concentrate on what I'm doing rather than looking around at the exposure and letting fear of falling paralyze me. I inhale deeply, and repeat, again and again until completed. During moments like these, there are no thoughts in my mind about what I need to do tomorrow, or what retirement looks like, or whether that particular person back home trusts my leadership. Poof! All worries are vaporized by the beauty and reality of living entirely in the present moment. Step. By. Step. Each successful step breeds a confidence that all will be well. And though the ladder is short and descending takes only a few seconds, those seconds are etched into my memory as beautiful seconds when I was governed by neither fear nor familiarity. "This," I think to myself, "is how I want to live"—breathing deeply, paying attention, fully alive to each moment.

The wise preacher who wrote the book of Ecclesiastes says, "Whatever your hand finds to do, do it with all your might, for in the realm of the dead, where you are going, there is neither working nor planning nor knowledge nor wisdom" (9:10 NIV). It's his way of saying that wherever you are, you should be all there, fully present in the moment, not worrying about yesterday's failure or successes, or tomorrow's possibilities. The past is gone. The future doesn't exist. Now is all you have, so wake up. Pay attention.

The challenge for many of us is that familiarity breeds boredom and mediocrity. Everything that was new once becomes old and familiar. The job that at one point had such a steep learning curve has become too easy, boring even. The marriage that was born in those nights when you walked Paris together or sipped coffee until the sun rose has now become predictable, as if there's nothing left to discover. Food? Your commute? Your holidays? At every turn, familiarity is at risk of breeding, if not contempt, at least boredom.

In every instance, it is important to note that familiarity isn't the real risk. The danger is that we allow familiarity to kill our capacity for joy, presence, and being "all in" each and every moment. I understand the danger too well. I'd known a measure of success over the past years as a pastor, speaker, and author. The high ground there is exposed, and the risks and consequences of falling are great. It's an extraordinarily dangerous place. Up there, we're tempted to turn to autopilot, to "mail it in," as the saying goes. The truth, though, is that there is no autopilot for leadership, or marriage, or parenting, or faith. Success is dangerous territory because, just as in mountaineering, it often is the folks with the most experience that fall fatally. Goran Kropp rode his bicycle from Sweden to Mount Everest, climbed alone to the summit, descended safely, and rode home too. His abilities and capacity were undisputed, even among the elite of the world. Yet on September 30, 2002, he died on a little seventy-five-foot crag in Washington State. He'd placed what climbers call "protection" in the rock, so that, if they fall, they won't fall all the way to the ground, but his protection failed—either due to faulty equipment or faulty place-ment, or both. We'll never know. What we do know is that the more you do something, the easier it is to overcome fear, and the more prone you are to a complacency found often in the midst of famili-arity. It's true whether you're climbing a rock face, leading a meeting, playing with your children, or engaging in conversation with your close friend or spouse. No longer afraid, you're now at risk of seri-ous missteps.

It doesn't need to be that way, though. Nurture an attitude of accepting the reality that wherever you are, whatever you're facing, this is where you need to be in the moment. Recognize that you have protection, that nothing this fallen world can throw at you will ever be able to steal the companionship you have with the deep wellspring of joy and hope that is Christ himself. And finally, pay attention to each glorious moment, because it's the only moment you have.

I entered sabbatical thinking that these were the most important lessons I'd learn. Truth be told, though, I already knew them, at least a bit, but I was simply failing to practice them. Some lessons that were even more important for me came from an unlikely source—not from rocks and ridges, but from people, as we'll see next.

Notes

[1] Photos for this chapter: http://bit.ly/Exposure8.

[2] The world is full of forgiveness stories that swim upstream, running contrary to our lust for revenge.

As We Forgive is a movie about the powerful reconciliation movement that's happened after the genocide. You can find it here: http://bit.ly/rwandaforgiving.

Major Ian Thomas, a British major involved in evangelism after WWII, picked up a German hitchhiker, introduced him to life in Christ, and eventually entrusted him with starting a ministry in Germany.

You can listen to a powerful story of the Amish community forgiving the mother of a man who killed several young girls in an Amish school house ten years ago. The link is: http://bit.ly/amishforgiving.

[3] I'll share greater detail of this story in Chapter Fourteen.

PEOPLE

The greatest single cause of atheism in the world today is Christians: who acknowledge Jesus with their lips, walk out the door, and deny Him by their lifestyle. That is what an unbelieving world simply finds unbelievable.

—Brennen Manning

I pray that you will understand the words of Jesus, "Love one another as I have loved you." Ask yourself, "How has he loved me? Do I really love others in the same way?" Unless this love is among us, we can kill ourselves with work and it will only be work, not love. Work without love is slavery.

—Mother Teresa

And if anyone gives even a cup of cold water to one of these little ones who is my disciple, truly I tell you, that person will certainly not lose their reward.

—Jesus the Christ (Matt. 10:42 NIV)

The original plan was to trek alone, maybe with a few friends at various times along the way. The stated reason for this had to do with a deeply held belief of mine that I'm never alone, even when I'm alone. When I tell people I'm going here or there to speak at some event, they ask me if my wife's going. When I say no, they ask, "So you're going alone then?" To which I reply, "I never travel alone." Trains, planes, long drives, long walks, nights out in the high country under the stars, I've done all of them "by myself," but not really because I know the very real experience of companionship with Christ, a companionship that's as real to me as any human friendship. I point to Jesus as my example, because he liked to head off by himself to pray.[1]

Years ago, I was in conversation with a friend in my office. We were talking about God and people, and I said that I had a hard time trusting people, that God was my "go to" for companionship and friendship. She was stunned, saying that she found people so much more reliable than God.

"People die," I said.

"God sits by passively and watches us suffer rather than intervene," she explained.

"Yes, but we suffer at the hands of people, not God," I countered. "Abuse, betrayal, infidelity."

"Earthquakes? Plagues? Fires?" she said. "We suffer at the hands of God."

"Yes, but God comforts us in the midst of all this tragedy, along with the pain we experience when people betray us or leave us."

It went on like this for a while, a philosophical stalemate. There was conviction behind our respective views, but there was also a story for each of us that shaped our views. My story included plenty of loss and abandonment: I was given up for adoption shortly after birth; a good friend my age was killed by a drunk driver running a red light when I was sixteen; my grandparents all died before I turned nineteen; my favorite aunt died suddenly while on the operating table for a minor procedure when I was twenty. She'd invited me over for lunch the day before her surgery, but I told her I had a big project due for an architecture class, that I'd see her after the surgery. "After" never happened. My sister died of a sudden heart attack when she was forty-two. My friend and close coworker, the main associate pastor at the church I lead, died of cancer in his forties.

People? Even if they want to be there for you, death always wins, and those we love exit the stage, too early for my liking, at least in all the cases above. Let's not even get started talking about the people who let you down, especially the people who appear super-spiritual to the outside world, but who, on the inside, have huge landscapes of greed, or anger, or insecurity, or lust that continue unchecked. Trust? No thanks. I'll take my chances with God instead.

All of this, coupled with my introverted personality, led to the creation of a life-rhythm I enjoy, which includes engagement with people and then withdrawal to be alone. I like both sides of this equation, and genuinely like being with people. Still, if I'm honest, I'd say that I find the "alone" part to frequently be more life-giving. Does this mean I didn't want to do this trek with my wife? Not at all! Once she expressed interest in joining me, we had this very conversation, and I said, "Don't worry, honey. Hiking with you is just like hiking alone"—which I don't necessarily recommend saying to your spouse if you want to win points, though in our case she took it as a compliment. Donna's safe. My relationship with her is more life-giving to me than any other in my world. That I can say this about my spouse makes me profoundly grateful and is testimony to her grace, patience, good humor, and adaptability.

What I wasn't so keen on was the notion of spending night after night in huts, eating and even sleeping with strangers. "We'll need to talk with them," I moaned. My vision for this trip was heavy on silence and solitude. I was on the hunt for revelation from God and restoration, but I'd presumed these things would come from nights under the Milky Way, and the awe, beauty, and power of raw creation delivered uncensored from the earth and skies, not from people.

August 5. Italy. *Having found that there are no vacancies in our planned huts for the upcoming days, we decided to hike out of the high country, down into the valley, in search of a place to spend the night while we retooled our route for Italy. "Italy is full" is the message we received often enough that we began to believe it. But in the midst of our search for lodging, two encounters happened that would challenge my practice of faith and change the way I pray—and live.*

The first one came in the town of Wellsberg. We'd spent most of the day hiking to get there, with the thought that since this was the largest town around, we'd surely find some lodging. Arriving at about 3 P.M. and seeing that the Tourist Information office didn't reopen 'til 4, I decided to walk through town and check out lodging options. "Full." "Tutto Completo." "L'Italia è piena." "Italy is full." How many ways can you say it?

In the midst of this orgy of rejection, though, one guest-house was mentioned several times. "If anyone can make room for you, it will be _____." I felt as if I were Jean Valjean, looking for a place to lay my head for the night, and everyone kept saying, "You haven't tried there . . . ," while pointing to this particular guest house.

*I made my way there before the Information center
opened, and though the front door was wide open and the
place filled with guests, there seemed to be no host. I noted
a cross, a candle, and a picture of Pope Francis in the entry-
way, common decor in Italy. After the Information center
also said, "You need to try there . . . ," pointing in that direction, we decided it was worth going back and seeing, at the
least, why everyone spoke so highly of it.*

*We knock, and a woman opens the door—a woman who
looks like Mother Teresa, with gray hair crowning her diminutive Italian frame. She speaks only German and Italian,
not a word of English, but my daughter speaks German, so
she tells the woman of our plight. It's late afternoon by now,
and I'm beginning to wonder if there's shelter anywhere. The
woman, in spite of the language barrier, exudes joy and
seems genuinely glad to see us.*

*She takes my daughter's hand and overflows with com-
passion, even as she tells us that she has no room for us. She
tells us how she'd love to provide shelter for us if she could,
but that it's impossible, that there's not a bed to be found. Her
sympathy for our plight is evident, almost as if we are her
own children and she is telling us that she's lent our bedroom
out to guests, as if she had a room just for us that is, sadly,
occupied. She wishes us well, and we know she means it.*

*She closes the door, and the three of us look at each other,
filled and deeply moved by the weight of her love and mercy.
"What just happened?" we say to each other.*

"I think we just met Jesus," I respond as we walk on.

Indeed. Though some will argue with the imprecision of my theological language, the truth is that this woman embodied the spirit of

Christ. We encountered the love, compassion, and hospitality of Jesus as this woman's countenance and response transcended the barrier of language, and even the barrier of her being unable to meet our needs. We were "blessed"—it's the only word that works—by her presence. This blessing would become a holy haunting through the rest of the trip. But our day wasn't finished.

Having found no lodging in the big town of Wellsberg, we jump on a train and make our way back to Schmeiden, a smaller town where we'd stopped for lunch. We'd seen a few "Zimmer" signs, so we hope there might be a single room for the three of us somewhere. Nope. Wrong again. By now it's nearly 6 P.M., so the girls scurry to the Visitor Center, arriving just before it closes, while I make my way to another guesthouse sign, where I again learn "Italy is full." I catch up with them outside the Visitor Center, now closed. They have two phone numbers in their possession, where the Visitor Center computer has told them there are two rooms available. One room's within walking distance, and the other is 8km away, about halfway back up the mountain where we'd hiked out today. It's late enough by now, though, that no busses are heading up there, and the village is small enough that there are no cabs, so this one, too, will need to be walking distance, in spite of the fact that we've already walked 18km today and are utterly spent.

First call. "Oh, I'm sorry. I just finished talking with someone, and they booked the room. We're full." Second call. The woman speaks much more Italian than German, and no English at all, so our daughter "thinks" we have a room, but isn't quite certain. This is good news, other than the fact that the 8km hike back uphill will likely take us two and a half hours and it's 6:30 now, and the last busses have already left, there are no taxis, and we're hungry and tired. The thought of walking back, uphill, for 8km, in this condition sounds dreadful.

Still, I'm stoic enough that I can press on and do just about anything other than ask for help. After all, "It's my mess—it's my responsibility to fix it."

"Let's go," I say, adding, "no point whining about it—it must be done." While my daughter and I are putting our packs back on, Donna sees a couple returning from a restaurant next door to the now closed tourist office. They've gotten in their car with German license plates and were ready to start their engine, when Donna walks right up to the window on the passenger side and knocks on it. I'm horrified. Is she going to do what I think she's going to do? Is she going to ask total strangers, foreigners even, for help?

The middle-aged, well-dressed woman, rolls down the window. I watch and listen as Donna says, "Do you speak English?"

"Yes," she says. I can't tell if her smile is warmth or hidden fear.

"Well, we've been hiking all day looking for lodging but haven't been able to find anything. We've just found a room, but it's back up in the river valley where we came from, and it's late, and we're hungry. Would you please give us a ride?"

Is she really doing this? Asking a stranger for a ride? Asking someone to inconvenience themselves on our behalf? Yes. She's doing this, and the reason she's willing to do this is because my dear wife of so many years has lived her life being willing to be inconvenienced in order to help others. She's energized by helping people in need, often at cost to *herself. She picks up other people's garbage. She visits people in the hospital. She, if the roles were reversed, would give the ride. So she's able to ask for the ride.*

I fear I'd be too busy to give the ride (you know, busy: with team-building exercises, management responsibilities, study, prayer, and preaching a sermon about service and hospitality). I fear I'd be too judgmental to give the ride ("That's a bit of poor planning don't you think? And now you want me to backfill for you? Maybe it's better you suffer a bit so that you learn your lesson well and call ahead—don't want to go enabling your dysfunction now, do we?" You know the language. Maybe you've used it). I know myself. Because I wouldn't give the ride, I wouldn't ask for the ride.

The woman looks at her husband and they exchange a few words in German, and she says, "Of course. We'd be glad to." The husband's countenance changes, his face lighting up with joy as he gets out of the car and opens the trunk, shifting things around a bit to make room for our three packs, while he says, "We're hikers too. We understand." And so it was that our lives intersected with a delightful and generous couple from northern Germany who'd come down to Italy for a holiday.

The 8km journey takes about ten minutes instead of two and a half hours. The two hug us, tell us they were delighted to give us this ride, and then drive back, disappearing down the valley to the lodging they'd reserved months in advance. We're greeted at this thoroughly Italian inn by the woman who'd spoken with our daughter Kristi on the phone. She welcomes us with hugs and the word that we are "just in time for supper," which is delightful news. We enjoy a feast of fresh greens, prosciutto on melon, and a pasta dish whose pleasure to the palate is nearly orgasmic, filled with spinach and cheese, along with mashed potatoes and something dipped in tempura batter. And to think we could have been hiking uphill on empty stomachs all this time, instead, were it not for the kindness of strangers and my wife's humble courage to ask for help. The sky is clear, the air crisp, and I fall into a deep and contented sleep right after supper, humbled by hospitality and grace, by generosity and free rides.

Back in Seattle, alone, on training hikes and in the upstairs office of my house where most of the planning for this trip unfolded, I was certain that God would speak to me during this precious sabbatical time, but I'd assumed it would be through the majesty and breathless beauty of creation, and through the lessons learned by walking. I presumed I'd learn lots of things about endurance and risk, navigation and faith. Yes, those lessons would be there, but in truth I needed other lessons, lessons that can only be learned through people.

In 1 Kings 19, the mighty prophet Elijah is weary, battle worn, and on the run. At God's command, he's standing on top of a mountain, waiting for revelation from God. He has his own set of expectations regarding how God will "show up" for him, and it will, no doubt, be in a way that corresponds to his own personality. Will fiery Elijah find God in the mighty wind, or the earthquake, or the fire? Nope. He'll find the voice of God in the stillness of a gentle breeze, or in my case, in the hospitality of some middle-aged Germans and the owner of a guesthouse whose joy and compassion remind me of Jesus.

When God meets Elijah in the gentle wind, he asks him a simple question: "What are you doing here, Elijah?" And now, as I drift to sleep in this charming Italian inn, I ponder the same question. I wonder what I'm doing here in Europe this summer, what I'm doing with this precious time of sabbatical.

Like Elijah, I'm tired. But I'm not tired of preaching and teaching, and I thought I'd come here to discover a way to do more of that and less of the stuff I don't like. Maybe. But tonight, in the silent night of this precious gift of a room, I'm thinking that God's inviting me, before I think about doing different stuff, to become a different person. There are gaps in my faith that I see with greater clarity tonight than I've ever seen them in my life, shaken awake by this fresh context.

The woman who offered us no room with such love is a stark contrast to Pastor Richard when he sees yet another homeless person sleeping on the porch of "his" church building, or another person in need at the door. He's too busy, too guarded, too likely to give them what they ask for (a bag of food, or a referral number for lodging) rather than what they need (compassion and a sense that someone in this cold and lonely world actually cares about their well-being, even if that someone doesn't have "room" to help them).

The couple who offered us a ride are a contrast, too, to the Pastor Richard who makes every effort to run his life in a self-sufficient manner. Take care of yourself, and expect others to do the same. If this is what Jesus looks like, then the paralyzed guy by the pool dies by the pool without ever walking. The woman caught in adultery dies in a pool of her own blood, with her lesson learned, and a good warning for the rest of us from the first-century version of the Taliban who used, not the Qur'an, but the Bible to justify their killings. The leper is still in his colony, and the mad man is still roaming around in the tombs, terrorizing anyone who comes to visit their dead. If I only step in with solidarity for those who are worthy, I don't step in at all, and nobody steps in for me either. Faith in such a setting is reduced to personal piety. The fruit of it isn't love though; it's pride, self-sufficiency, and a judgmental mentality. It misrepresents Jesus, gets ugly fast, and is often woven deceptively into the fabric of our faith.

All this is utterly the opposite of the gospel; and when I think this way, prioritize this way, act this way, I'm not Jean Valjean, the man of grace in *Les Miserables*. I'm Javert, the legalistic, moral, upstanding religious citizen who'll keep the world clean. What's most insidious about this is that these gods of self-righteousness and moralism are all the harder to see because I swim in an ocean of God-talk and grace-talk and Jesus-talk every single day.

This is the danger of what I do, what we who follow Christ—or claim to—do every day, especially on Sundays. As I write this chapter, fear is saturating the globe because of the threat of an Islamic group that's beheading children, journalists, even mountain guides, in their attempt to conquer some land and build a pure Islamic state. Everyone's wondering how to stop them. One writer, Preston Sprinkle, though, had the courage to fly a little higher, above this immediate issue, and ask some bigger questions. Sprinkle wrote the following in his blog:

> Destroying ISIS is not the same as destroying evil. America could nuke every terrorist to hell and Satan would walk away untouched. Satan doesn't need ISIS. Perhaps he's using them, but I suspect he's putting more energy—as an angel of light—into moralistic, consumer driven, power hungry religious movements that are covered in a thin veneer of Christianity.[2]

Yes. The greater dangers are usually the subtle ones. The greater danger is that beneath our veneers of spirituality, we've completely bought into the gods of materialism and individualism, and in place of mature faith, we've substituted church attendance, Bible reading, and avoiding a few key sins (sexual sin, drunkenness, and anything that'll get you arrested). In such a subtly twisted model, churches can grow, pastors can preach, ministries can busy themselves, and it can all be good—so good in fact that our own success becomes the justification for our methods and the vindication of our maturity.

Then we meet a diminutive woman in Italy who smiles and holds our hands. We get a ride from strangers. We encounter someone we've lived with for thirty-five years who has the humility to ask a favor. We eat at the table of a woman whose laughing eyes and joyful hospitality transcend language barriers. And then I see it. However far I've come in my knowledge and preaching skills, I've got a ways still to go before I look like Jesus.

Notes

[1] Photos for this chapter: http://bit.ly/People9.

[2] Preston Sprinkle, "A Christian Response to ISIS," *Theology in the Raw,* October 2, 2014, http://www.patheos.com/blogs/theologyintheraw/2014/10/a-christian-response-to-isis/.

SHELTER

CHAPTER TEN

All we ever wanted was to come in from the cold.

—Joni Mitchell

Come to me . . . and I will give you rest.

—Jesus the Christ (Matt. 11:28 NIV)

Humanity is thin-skinned, and this is why we're on a perpetual quest for climate-controlled environments. We don't do well in extreme heat or cold, and as a result, we're looking for warmth whenever cold weather ignites in us a quest for heat. Our history in cold climates has tapestries on the walls, drapes on the windows, hot water bottles in the bed, and the radical notion of bringing fire indoors, all in our pursuit of creating habitable space when it's chilly.[1]

August 13. Trail to Bins Alm. *It's raining. Constantly. We'd heard that summer rains are common in the Alps, but as I shared elsewhere, my eagerness to pack light means my protection from exposure and rain consists of precisely one thin poncho, one thin, non-waterproof sweater, and one thin, non-waterproof jacket. Oh, and one more thing. The day I was packing, I couldn't find my warm base layer. Because I couldn't find it, I tossed a recently purchased, but never used, base layer in my pack instead, as I thought to myself,* No problem—this one's even lighter! *I was more than a little proud of my pack weight, which, fully loaded, came in at less than twenty pounds! I can walk with this thing forever, I thought, while standing on a scale at home on a perfect summer Seattle day of sunshine and 73 degrees.*

But now it's reality. The sun's not shining at all and won't, perhaps ever again—or so it feels. Every step higher is a step toward wetter and colder weather. It's on this two-hour jaunt

toward a locally famous farmhouse that I make a sorry discovery. The base layer I've brought is precisely the opposite
of my wool winter version. Rather than wicking sweat away
from the body, I've packed a shirt that's intended to "cool you
down" by holding the moisture in, near your body. It turns
out it's designed for running marathons on hot days, perfect
for keeping you wet and cool.

I learn this first because, for some reason, I'm finding
it impossible to stay warm on this leg of our trip. If I could
draw a cartoon of getting cold, it would begin at the outer
regions of the body, hands and feet, and slowly but inexorably spread toward the very center of my being. When this
happens slowly, it can go on for quite some time imperceptibly. This is the way of it that morning as I feel cold, but
mostly just sluggish. I really don't know what is wrong as we
see the farmhouse out in the distance, silhouetted through
the fog. We smell smoke from the fire first, then see the out-
line, and eventually the sign. We'd been told to stop there
because their cheese is famous, at least locally, and the way I
am feeling, we agree that stopping is a good idea.

As we stand outside the door, removing our packs followed by that thin film of nylon known as a "poncho," a local
farmer approaches. Instantly, I covet everything he's wearing: a thick wool sweater under an even thicker wool poncho,
tall leather boots, a wide-brimmed hat (likely wool too), and
a thick greying beard. He looks warm, and it is only then, by
contrast, that I begin to realize how cold I am. It's here, while
looking at him, that I realize the layer closest to my body is
sopping wet, that my inner "wicking" layer of clothing is in
desperate need of being wrung out. I've no alternative layer,
though, as I'd chosen to go minimalist.

> *Seconds later, the dawning realization of how cold I am hits me with still fuller force because, when we step inside, it is as if we've entered another world, stepping through some sort of Narnian wardrobe in reverse, or the Matrix, or a black hole whose gravity has sucked us into a different universe. Pick your metaphor—they all mean the same thing. The warm fire, laughing children, soup on the stove, even the glow of the lights, conspire to create a world so different that only then do I fully realize just how cold I am. I take the thin "reverse wicking" shirt off and hang it by the fire in hope of drying and warming it, secretly hoping that perhaps it catches fire so I never need to wear it again. Then I inhale and relax, letting the warmth wrap its arms around me like a hug.*

Humanity's pursuit of a life-sustaining comfort zone has its moral and spiritual parallel, as poets and songwriters down through the ages have attested. A favorite folk artist Joni Mitchell wrote a song, "Come in from the Cold," where she recalls her life in the fifties, a time of high school and sexual awakening, followed by the sixties with its protest songs and cries for peace, and then her achievement of fame. At every point, there's an aching for life to be more whole than it is, and especially to be a place of safety and intimacy. She describes this ache as a longing to "come in from the cold."[2]

Shakespeare said it centuries earlier in *King Lear* when he wrote,

> Poor naked wretches, wheresoe'er you are, that bide the
> pelting of this pitiless storm. How shall your houseless
> heads and unfed sides, your loop'd and window'd
> raggedness, defend you from seasons such as these?[3]

What Joni and William are saying is that all of us are cold. We're out there in the storm that is our life with not enough on, at least some of the time, and when this happens, a longing rises up in us to get warm, find shelter, add a layer. It's more than, "I'm not comfortable." It's a deep ache, like being cold, which will only be fixed with a dose of intimacy, or safety, or meaning.

The vulnerability of being cold is terrifying, almost like being naked. One author, in fact, says as much when he writes,

> Beneath our clothes, our reputations, our pretensions, beneath our religion or lack of it, we are all vulnerable both to the storm without and to the storm within, and if ever we are to find true shelter, it is with the recognition of our tragic nakedness that we have to start.[4]

This message, of course, stands in utter contrast to the notion of being the strong one. In alpine terms, there are the rescuers, with plenty of reserve in their lungs and muscles. They're warm and fed and able to go out and find the cold and hungry and bring them in. Most of us want to be the rescuers, of course, rather than *the rescued*, for the obvious reason that strength is better than weakness.

It's right here, though, that we religious professionals get it wrong at least half the time, because we think to ourselves that unless we're strong, we're weak. So our legitimate desire to be the rescuers leads us at times to put on masks, pretending to be holier or wiser or more powerful spiritually than we really are.

What's even worse is that sometimes we begin to believe it, begin thinking our masks are our reality. When that happens, we don't even know we're cold anymore, because we've shut off all the sensitivities that would make us aware of our own vulnerability. We are tired, but refuse to admit it. We have a fair dose of bitterness, or lust (for bodies in some cases, but also lusts for approval, or success, or a wide sphere of influence instead—lust wears many costumes), or petty cynicism in our own hearts, but can no longer see it. We're vulnerable too, and cold, but we're paid to be strong, so we pretend. We put on our holy face and walk into the crowd with answers, and joy, and power—not real ingredients rising from a full heart but, at least sometimes, fabrications that arise from our need to be more than we really are.

Rubbish. We—all of us—have days when we're naked and it's cold. I think one of the things that wears on people of faith, and especially on religious professionals, is the false notion that they must always be the ones with the answers, that they're always the strong ones. I grew up going to hospitals because my dad had an annual rendezvous with pneumonia. I hated those places because, though they could help him get over the acute infection, his lungs were weak and they couldn't do a thing to fix it. This meant that he, an athlete in college, was forced into an early retirement because he couldn't walk fifty yards without the exhaustion most folks feel after running a mile. Hospitals were an annual reminder that life's not fair, a testimony to how fragile life really is.

When I was seventeen, he went in for his annual flu shot in early October, standard fare for most of us. But he was just weak enough that it plunged him into sickness, which became pneumonia, which filled his lungs with fluid, which killed him. That sent me into a spiral of depression and a sort of irrational hatred of hospitals.

Fast forward thirty years and I'm now a pastor in a big urban church. A dear friend has cancer, so I'm going to visit her during her chemo treatments. I park the car, walk through the big hospital doors, find her floor, and head down the hall. When I walk into the room and see her sitting in a chair with tubes of ostensibly life-giving poison dripping into her body, my distaste for hospitals and the loss that ensues when health declines comes rushing back.

Within the span of maybe five seconds, an internal dialogue ensues in my head between "real me" and "pastor me":

Pastor me: "Be strong, give hope, have answers."
Real me: "I'm not strong, and I don't have answers."
Pastor me: "If you don't have answers, you can't help."
Real me: "Is it better to make up answers or to share my own questions?"

Pastor me: "You have answers. They're in the Bible. Come on. They're looking to you."
Real me: "But I don't buy it. I don't understand the promises of healing, at least not here, not now. I don't. All I can give them is who I am."

And with that, I dismiss the pastor voice, take my pastor hat off, and throw my arms around my friend as tears begin to flow. "I'm so sorry this is happening to you," is all I can say as she and her husband assure me all will be well, that the chemo will surely do its work. We pray together, laugh a bit, share some stories, and then I leave the room, wondering if what I've just done wasn't the biggest pastoral care-fail ever.

In retrospect, no. Jesus stands at the tomb of Lazarus and weeps. They're tears of anger, because Jesus, like the rest of us, hates the intrusion of death and suffering in this terribly broken and fallen world. He knows he'll raise this guy from the dead, knows there'll be great rejoicing, knows the end of the story. But even knowing all that, he offers us a glimpse into the reality of his humanity because he weeps. Here's a grown man crying, making a scene of it. I think he's trying to tell us something.

It's a cold world, and because we're thin-skinned, we're cold ourselves at times, longing for warmth. That's the point of it, I think. Jesus reminds us that on certain days, it's cold enough to make us weep. There are macro problems like racism, terror, seemingly spontaneous eruptions of economic volcanoes, and acts of war. Also, woven into the same fabric are our own personal threads. Babies die. Spouses cheat. Marriages and jobs get stale and an ache grows in our hearts. Money gets tight. Some harbor secret addictions that not only suck the life out of them from the energy spent hiding it, but also add weights of shame and guilt on top of them. It's a cold world, and we are, at least some of time, shivering.

Admitting I'm cold is surely the first step toward finding shelter. It's okay, in other words, to have longings, to be sad, weak, even angry. A quick survey of Psalms reveals that David, Asaph, Moses, and likely all the other true heroes of robust authentic faith knew this. They had strength, and surely they had seasons when they were the search-and-rescue team, seeking and saving, giving and pouring out. But God knows, and we do too, that they had their times of doubt and loneliness, fear and lust, failure and sickness. They had times of an aching longing for their world, and for the bigger world too, to be better than it was.

"I'm the cold one here, and the whining one too," I think to myself as I look at my wife on the trail, as happy and easy-going as ever. "All this Bible study and prayer, all this teaching and preaching, all this leading and serving I do, and she's got the winning attitude; she's the strong one. What's up with that?" I'm mad about that for at least half a mile because I like recipes: a dash of prayer, a pinch of Bible study; sprinkle with a little repentance, and presto! Holiness, ready to serve up to a broken world. You'll rejoice in tribulation and suffering, love your enemies, conquer fear and lust, and basically look like Jesus.

This formulaic approach is of the devil, because it creates in us a sense of false guilt when things don't go well, and as a result, many of us end up pretending things are fine when we're dying inside. How odd that the Christian subculture, intended to lead us into a life of freedom and authenticity, should so very often become a petri dish in which the germs of hypocrisy thrive.

Reality and true truth are utterly other than this sham performance. Finding them begins, nearly always, with the acknowledgment that sometimes we're cold. Not generically cold, but cold because of the storms of life, or because we've made bad decisions, like packing a shirt that's intended to cool rather than warm, and then hiking in a thirty-seven-degree rainstorm. Acknowledging I was cold led, in the short term, to our choice to stop for lunch and, in the long term, to a stepped-up wardrobe, but it all began with the simple realization that

I'd made poor choices and was suffering because of it. I pray that this kind of honest authenticity can bleed into the rest of my life.

Bins Alm to Lamsenjochhütte. *After a lunch of hot soup and amazing, fresh cheese, it's time to leave the comfort of the Bins Alm farm and continue hiking higher. I don't want to go anywhere—not because I'm cold, but because I'm now warm. This newfound warmth has filled me with a comfort that's intoxicating, addicting even. I look out the window at howling winds and rain, and every fiber of my being resists going. But go we must, because we came here to experience all aspects of the trek and learn whatever we can from every single step. These next steps wouldn't be ones I'd choose, but we must take them.*

I put the inner layer on again, now mostly dry, thanks to the fire. The poncho, though, is wet and cold. Same with the pack. Same with the hat. Same with everything. Wet. And cold. For some reason (likely having to do with my wife's love of the outdoors, and her superior planning skills, and her outdoor recreation major brain, molded and shaped to love suffering by virtue of the many hiking classes she took), Donna is unaffected by all this. She's smiling, stoic, and ready to hike. Ready or not, I follow her out the door into the exposure.

We make our way higher, and as we do, the air gets still colder. Our goal is Lamsenjochhütte, at 1,953 meters (about six thousand feet), and it takes us most of the afternoon to find our way there. "Find our way" is operative here, because there's a point during this journey when we're hiking in the clouds, and there's no visibility between the previous trail marker and the pass we know is somewhere ahead of us. During this time, there are options. Various stream beds with water running in them pose as trails. Which one to take? We really don't know, but compass and altimeter become our truth-tellers so that, at the least, we know we're headed in the right direction and approaching the pass.

Soon the pass comes into view through emptying clouds that are our world in these moments. Within minutes, we see not only the pass, but the trail-marker sign at the pass, a wooden pole on which various signs point to various trails. This, we know, confirms our direction as proper, so I pick up my pace a bit. I'm cold, but no colder than I was on the way to Bins Alm earlier this morning. I know that from the pass, it's less than an hour to our destination, so I'm feeling good about the whole day. The end is in sight. Cold. But good.

Once we arrive at the pass, though, everything changes. We're greeted there by steady winds of perhaps thirty miles per hour, and this makes my already pitiful poncho worthless, perhaps even a liability. It begins dancing in the wind, and as it does, I feel cold water pouring down my back from the hood. I'd forgotten to put the hood up, but now I think it wise to do so in light of the wind. Unfortunately, it has collected water during the ascent, which pours down my back —like what happens to coaches when they win football games.

None of this is happening to Donna who, of course, wore her hood properly the whole time. In fact, in her diary from this day, she writes, "I feel uniquely strong. Reflecting on our Italy trip fifteen years ago, I realize that back then, at forty, I felt as if I were fifty-five. Now, at fifty-five, I feel as if I'm forty!" She continues, "Richard, however . . ."

Yes, I'm the one with problems. Soon after reaching the pass, I begin to shiver, something I don't think I've done since

*I was four. My hands grow achingly numb. When Donna asks
me a question and my speech is a bit slurred in my response,
I know what's happening. I'm in the early stages of hypothermia. The bone-sucking cold is doing a number on me. When
that happens, you become obsessed with getting warm. The
only warmth in this particular equation is that which will be
found in Lamsenjochhütte, so I quicken my pace.*

*"Must get there," I say to myself, "as soon as possible." It's
not visible yet, but the map tells me it's close. Joch means
"high mountain pass," so this means we're hiking still higher,
still colder, every step of the way. Donna is stopping to take
pictures of black salamanders she sees on the trail. She's smiling, happy, leisurely.*

*I'm possessed, lusting for warmth as if my life depends
on it. When the flags of the hut come into view, it appears
that we're still twenty minutes or so away from shelter, so I
quicken my pace. The trail is narrow and in places exposed,
with a steep five hundred-meter drop off to our left. This is
a nonissue for me as I move as fast as I can toward what I
know will be warmth and shelter. The cold that's stolen comfort from my body has reduced my world to only one single
consideration: I must get warm—as soon as possible.*

*I press on, and within minutes I'm at the door of
Lamsenjoch. The flags blowing outside are outstretched by
the relentless wind. The tables on the deck are drenched,
empty of the flowers, menus, and laughing, sunning guests
characteristic of better days. Once again, as soon as I step
inside, the healing begins. Check in. Head upstairs. Strip
off the wet and replace it with the dry. Roll out the bag and
crawl in, with a blanket tossed on top for good measure.
Thirty minutes later, it's hot chocolate. Thirty after that, it's*

pasta with cheese, bacon, and crispy onions woven through-out, and a glass of wine. Ten minutes later: Healed. Warm. Content. Shalom.

Waking up in the communal sleeping attic of Lamsenjoch, I ponder what's just happened. "The good news called 'gospel' is nothing, if not an invitation to shelter—having the humility to know I need it, the guts to seek it, and the generosity to share it with others whenever its mine to give.

The beauty of seeking shelter in the Alps is that there aren't many options. There are huts. And nothing else. Tents are so strongly discouraged that we didn't even bring one, and the truth is that Alps hikers are geared for a substantial shelter, a hut, at the end of each day. We're all unprepared to stay outside overnight, and this is why everyone's intent on getting there, because there's shelter or facing the elements, warmth or cold, hot drinks or maybe water if you can find a stream or lake. When the choices are painted that clearly, it's easy to choose wisely. It's press on to the hut or get stuck out in the cold.

Back in real life, though, it's alarmingly easy to stay outside in the cold of isolation, bitterness, fear, or addiction, even while I say, "I'm fine; thanks. You?" as I shiver under my meager covering. Maybe it's time we recognize that both finding and giving shelter is the first and best thing we can do sometimes. After all, all we ever wanted was to come in from the cold.

Notes

[1] Photos for this chapter: http://bit.ly/Shelter10.

[2] Joni Mitchell, "Come in from the Cold," © Sony/ATV Music Publishing LLC, Crazy Crow Music / Siquomb Music Publishing, http://bit.ly/mapnotjourneyshelter.

[3] From *King Lear*, Act III, quoted in *Telling the Truth*, by Frederic Beuchner (New York City: Harper and Row, 1977), 29.

[4] Ibid., 33.

ENDURANCE

CHAPTER ELEVEN

I will cling to the rope God has thrown me in Jesus Christ,
even when my numb hands can no longer feel it.

—Sophie Scholl

If you have run with footmen and they have tired you out,
then how can you compete with horses?

—Jeremiah 12:5

147

In preparation for our grand adventure, I purchased a book called *Training for the New Alpinism*. It provided all the latest science about how to turn your human body into an endurance machine. By the time I finished reading the book, I knew that preparation was simple: I needed to do a lot of long-distance walking with my pack on and some slow jogging without it. I learned I'd be served best by this if I did it consistently enough to continually increase distances, all the way up until a few days before our departure. All these hours, I learned from the wisdom of science, would pay off. By the end of those workouts, I'd have a body able to go the distance and fast enough to arrive before nightfall.[1]

This last point about nightfall was, in the beginning, a real motivator for the fitness regime. Unlike the wilds of the American west where you can pitch your tent pretty much anywhere you like on Forest Service land, Europe was going to be entirely "hut to hut" in keeping with their cultural mores. In America, backpacking allows the freedom to stop almost any time. "Are you tired? Cold? Wet from the rain? Well, then, why are you still walking when you can stop, pitch your tent, crawl into your bag, and sleep? No need to keep moving. You can start rest. Now!" There'd be none of that luxury in Europe. We had read the trail guide and realized that some days could be as many as thirty kilometers, with stopping before reaching our intended destination not an option.

The other motivator for a fitness regime was my age. At fifty-eight, I didn't have many friends thinking about doing this kind of thing. A few have some recreation in their lives—a little skiing, a little walking or running, mountain biking, maybe a hike now and then. None of them, though, were pondering forty days of trekking. The only people I knew of who did this were people I'd read about in magazines. They seemed larger than life, able to go the distance because of rare genetic gifts and a lifetime of training. This left me, a mere mortal, wondering if I'd have what it takes to finish.

I had solid reasons for my self doubts, because a couple of years ago, my wife and I planned for a spring ascent of Mt. St. Helens (of eruption fame) on snowshoes. We prepared for it with some short hikes and a little circuit training for a few months. We also got our butts kicked, turning back a few hundred feet from the summit due to exhaustion. The lessons learned in that failure, though, were priceless.

I'd learned then that you can think you're prepared for something, but you never really know until you take the journey. This is as true in the rest of life as it is with trekking, maybe more so. Few people, if any at all, who utter the words "'til death do us part" during their wedding believe they won't go the distance. "Only a fool starts building a house without having the resources to finish it," is how Jesus put the same thing, which is his way of saying that we should favor sobriety over flippancy when it comes to assessments of our own abilities, especially our abilities to finish what we start.

August 18. *This is a long day, hiking from Garmish to Linderhof in Germany. We set out following the signs, and the trail runs immediately adjacent to a highway for several kilometers before turning off and heading north into the forest and up. These are lowlands, foothills. It's warm, and it's made warmer still by the knowledge that much of the day will be spent in ascent. As has happened so often on our trek, it's a morning of up, up, and more up, but today the air is thick with humidity, feeling more like Philadelphia than the Alps. This means more body heat, more sweat, more loss of* *strength per step than we'd experienced on any previous day. After an hour of this, Donna and I do for each other what we did for our children when they were small and grew tired of hiking; we broke the hike up into tiny pieces. "Let's stop for water at the next curve." "Okay. Three more curves and we'll stop to catch our breath again." "Up there, where it looks like there's a bridge and stream. That's where we'll stop for lunch."*

This will be one of our longest days. Long is relative, of course. Near our home in Washington State, we often encounter hikers on the Pacific Crest Trail (PCT), a 2,659-mile jaunt that meanders through the Sierra Nevada, Siskou, and Cascade Mountains, from the border of Mexico all the way to Canada. Those seeking to go the distance usually start in the south and mail food drops to themselves via General Delivery at various post offices along the way. They have a timeframe that opens in April (where there'll likely still be plenty of snow in the high country of the Sierras) and closes in October when the Cascades begin receiving mighty storms as the moisture flowing in off the Pacific kisses the cold air of the north and quickly buries the high country in white stuff. To go the distance means most days will be twenty or more miles, and rest days will be few and far between.

Because we live near this trail, I encounter "thru-hikers," as they're called, on a regular basis during my morning runs or my visits to the gas station (which is also the post office) to pick up the mail. This summer, I met a man who was on his fifth pair of shoes, just as he'd reached the twenty-four-hundred-mile mark. He was nearing seventy years old, and this was his fourth time to hike the entire length of the trail.

We met a priest on our travels in Europe who had hiked his way from Jerusalem to Switzerland, racking up about five thousand km!

By comparison, our forty-day, four-hundred-km journey seemed like a desk job, hardly a speck on the endurance map, barely worthy of consideration. Still, endurance is relative, and for us, this trip as a whole, and certain days in particular, demanded from us levels of strength far outside our norms and comfort zones. This would stretch us and transform us, not only physically, but spiritually and emotionally too, as we learned the meaning, value, and ingredients of endurance.

August 28. Feldkirchhütte to Liechtenstein. *The day begins with an early breakfast because our hostess, knowing where we're heading, tells us it will be a "very long day," starting out in a westerly direction through some high alpine farms. The deep, rich mud, a product of the intensely rainy summer, doubles the weight of our shoes, and there are times when we unavoidably sink to our ankles. Again, as on a previous long day, it is exceptionally warm, and the cattle whose land we're visiting have left gifts where flies, gathered for conventions, are happy to visit our sweaty heads and necks for a change of menu. All this inconvenience is counterbalanced by a large farmer whose merriment and appreciation of hikers transcends language. From his farm, we can see Drei Schwestern ("Three Sisters"), a stunning trio of summits that marks the border between Liechtenstein and Austria.*

We ascend through the mud of the grazing land into a forest, as the trail gains elevation toward a ridge. Even here, the cattle have been in play, so the mud dance continues, along with the heat and flies. All of this slows our progress, and from the ridge we can see that we'll descend again, this time into sheep pasture, before another ascent to a different ridge. On the second ridge, we stop for lunch where the cooler air and a breeze coming up and over the ridge from Liechtenstein conspire to keep the flies away. This, coupled with the extreme steepness ahead of us, is enough justification to linger on the ridge for an extended lunch. We ponder the ascent still ahead of us today, up a ridge filled with exposure, cables, and rebar. It will be steep. And taxing. We're already hot. And tired. It's here we meet the priest who's walked to this mountain from Jerusalem, and while we dine, he's fit enough to take "a little side trip" to Drei Schwestern, ascending and descending before we finish our lunch. "He's younger," I say to myself, defensively, grasping for an explanation of the fact that he's faster, stronger, and fitter than me.

We finish our lunch and press on to the top, the cross at Garselikopf. It's a glorious peak from which we can see three countries without even turning our heads. The journey from the ridge to the summit, as anticipated, is tiring. The steepness and exposure conspire to create weariness and a wish that we could remain here at the top for the night. This, I realize, is in my nature. When I've arrived at a place that was costly to reach, my preference is to stay there for a while, to cherish the success and replenish before moving on. Today, though, as is so often the case in real life, that option isn't available. It's time to move.

We stop at the summit cross to enjoy the views and replenish electrolytes by putting magic tablets in our water bottles. From here, we can see that the trail will descend substantially before disappearing toward what we assume to be the headwaters of a river valley.

The descent is as harrowing as the ascent, more so actually, and by now it's mid-afternoon. Heat and weariness conspire, quickly taking the shine off the trip and turning many parts of the day into a requirement rather than the gift it is. Once off the dicey part of the ridge, the long traverse is easy except for the still-growing heat, warming moment by moment due to both the hour of the day and the loss of elevation. We're hot. We're tired. We've had enough. We want to stop.

That's when we turn the corner that had previously hidden the trail and see that it continues to descend slightly before a steep ascent once again, in order to leave Austria and finally cross the border into Liechtenstein.

We knew this, of course. We have maps. But knowing something on a map is vastly different from seeing the terrain left to gain when it's already 4 P.M. and you're hot, tired, and now rationing your water because you don't know when you'll find more. Disheartening is the right word for what we see, and yet we must press on, so we do—though we don't want to. It will be four more hours before we arrive at our lodging in Liechtenstein, and that time will include some accidental "off-trail" lostness, from which we recover only by running into a random retired member of the Liechtenstein cross-country ski team out for a stroll. He "talks us off the ledge," not metaphorically, but actually, because in our attempt to find a short cut, we have wandered onto a forested ridge, thick with downed trees and challenges. By the time we are in our room, the sun is long gone, and we eat alone in the dining room since all the other guests have finished supper. We'll sleep tonight, and tomorrow we'll do it all over again, whether we want to or not.

Endurance indeed!

Our trekking days, though peppered with conversation, gave us hundreds of hours to be alone in our thoughts, and I spent more than a few of them thinking about endurance. "God tricked me into becoming a pastor," is something I say sometimes, half kidding, but only half. I'd finished seminary with the intention of teaching at the college level. My first position had been signed and sealed at a small Bible college in Alaska. The position would start up in about year, but I was uncertain what to do in the meantime. That's when a church on a small island in Washington State called in search of an interim pastor. I said yes, and six months became six years, serving as their pastor, preaching weekly, and caring the growing flock. That yes was thirty years ago, and I've been in pastoral ministry the entirety of three decades, on an island, in a house church in the mountains, and now in a large urban setting.

As I hike these Alps, I'm about to finish my eighteenth year as the senior leader of a large church in Seattle, and my wife and I have been married almost twice that long. On our thirty-fifth wedding anniversary, we'll be hiking. And I'll not be celebrating the fact that we've "made it" and "hung in there" for all these years, but the reality that I love her more than ever and am more grateful now that I married her than the day I said "I do," "I will," and all those other blind promises brides and grooms make. Far from wearing us down, the years seem to have given us more life and love than ever. What a gift!

I still love my job as a pastor too, a job I nearly didn't take when it was offered almost two decades ago. These things are mysteries to me, because if you could look under the veneer of my longevity, you'd see moments of discouragement, especially in the early years when I desperately wanted to quit. You'd see frustrations related to my marriage, places where I felt stuck, or she did, or times when we both did. You'd see, too, canyons of boredom into which I'd inadvertently wandered, boredom which bred ugly thoughts and choices. And yet, somehow, we're here—celebrating longevity and endurance, even as our bodies on these particular days are screaming at us that the day is too long, the distance too far.

The benefits of endurance aren't readily apparent in an age of disposability and mobility. When things get hard, or boring, it appears that starting over is a default instinct, at least in our culture. Spouses, friendships, vocations, geographical loyalties, faith commitments—everything's disposable should "something better come along," or even "something different." Mindsets that feed our hyper-mobility have conspired to create a culture of loneliness, alienation, and a bent toward starting over.

Of course, there are times to move. Of course, there are necessary endings, and the needed courage to get out of an abusive situation or to draw a line in the sand. A sea of refugees are leaving their homes because the risk of death is nothing compared to the risk of remaining in their current hell, reminding us of this sad reality every day. But they leave because of beatings, torture, bombings, and systemic rape, not boredom or the inconvenience of needing to face a conflict honestly. For every person who should be leaving and doesn't, I'd suggest that there are many more who should stay and forgive, stay and have the hard conversation, stay and put in a little time with tedium and boredom, but don't. They, and you, and I, have need of endurance.

Endurance, it turns out, is a cocktail, requiring a blend of several key ingredients if we hope to see it develop in our lives. The lessons learned in acquiring the physical ability to "go the distance" for forty days find parallels for thriving in other significant areas of life.

Faith

The New Alpinism was my bible of training for our trek. I won't get into all the details of mitochondria, lactose buildup, fatigue phases, super-compensation phases, periodization, and so much more, other than to say there were lots of charts with objective data and a few stories from people who'd put the principles into practice. Now that I had read it, I could either believe it and put it into practice, or ignore it.

One of the particularly annoying realities of physical endurance is that it's gained slowly. The gains made are about as perceptible as watching hair grow, which is a way of saying "you won't feel a thing after your workouts, other than tired. But trust us. Subject yourself to hour after hour of this, and your capacity for moving farther faster will grow."

Now the ball's in my court, so to speak. Either I believe it or I don't, and the believing either results in a change of priorities on my part, or it doesn't. I decide to throw my lot in with science, and that's it. Time is carved out of full lives for hikes in the rain or sun, snow or heat. Rest and recovery are taken seriously too. Step by step. I don't feel a thing most of the time, or if I do feel, it's mostly just tired. Nevertheless, I do it, by faith, because someone tells me it's good for me.

It turns out that God has a training program too. It's called "trials." They have the effect of testing our faith, the way running tests muscles and skeletal structure. The testing, the pressing through when you feel like quitting, the continuing to show up, all of it changes you. Just as running increases your oxygen capacity, endurance in vocation, calling, and relationships creates increased capacities for things like love, forgiveness, service, contentment, and the willingness to be "all in," even on mundane days when life seems to offer nothing more than gray. These qualities can no more be learned through a book than you can become a marathoner by attending lectures and looking at slide shows of how the body works. Transformation doesn't happen in the classroom, it happens in the arena.

It's Abraham waiting twenty-five years for a child. It's David waiting decades for the throne after being anointed king. It's Joseph waiting for his dreams to come true. Marriage on the rocks, job that's far beneath your capacity though there are no signs of promotions on the horizon and a family to feed, a health crisis that drains your savings, vast numbers of people disappointed in you because you took a stand on an ethical issue, a car accident followed by months of disability and physical therapy. Endurance is clothed in every variety of trial. The important thing is to see it as a training program, to put our shoes on and get going. Such seeing, though, requires faith.

Gratitude and Presence

One of the ironies of trekking or hiking as a hobby is that there's a solid destination in mind almost all the time. You rise in the morning, look at your map, and set your sights on what's next. With a destination in mind, you load your pack, hoist it onto your back, and go.

If you've slept well, you'll start your day wide awake, aware, grateful even. You'll see and hear birds, and whether you know their official Audubon name or not, you'll absorb the sound and color. You'll stop and marvel at shelf fungus on trees, or the way light is torn into shafts by those same trees. You'll absorb the smell of wet, or dry, and hear the creek's dance long before you see it. This might go on for an hour, even two if you're good.

Long before you finish the day, though, you run the risk of becoming the walking dead. You're still moving, but you've fallen asleep, turning inward, more attune to bodily pains, hunger, sweat, and the annoyance of insects than to any revelations of beauty. A million disappointments occupy you, but these won't last long at all. Soon, instead of thinking about the present, you'll start thinking about the future, in particular your next destination. It will become an obsession if you let it, as you, with increasing volume, wish you were "there" instead of "here."

When this happens, it's only a few steps further until "here" becomes the enemy, a criminal whose only offense is its failure to be the destination. I see this often on the Pacific Crest Trail. From mid-August through the beginning of October, a daily parade of "thru hikers" pass by the trail near our house, as I've already mentioned. They can broadly be lumped into two categories. There's a minority who are still enjoying the journey, still seemingly alive and present to the glory of the mountains, still owning a capacity to stop and breathe in the scent, to let creation speak to their hearts.

The rest have become driven. Their situation is outwardly the same as those still enjoying the journey. Both groups are on the same trail, the same distance from the start, having endured the same weather, carried the same amount of weight, eaten mostly the same food. In spite of the vast similarities, though, for this last group, it has become a different journey entirely—no longer a treasure to be savored but an exercise in suffering to be done with as quickly as possible. They're essentially finished already, even though they have two hundred miles still ahead of them. With eyes looking straight down and a gait intent only on reaching the next destination, the capacity for enjoyment has vaporized like breath on a cold morning. The sooner it's over, the better.

You don't need trekking to know the feeling. We hop in the car, and when we hit the freeway that isn't moving, some of us can feel our blood pressure rising. Offended that the masses are presently conspiring to use the same road we want to, we're irritated, and this irritation quickly turns to anger when we see that all lanes around us have cars that are moving while we stand still. Yes, the sun's still shining on the bluest water. Yes, the clouds are still glorious, and the Space Needle stands tall at the south end of a cityscape that is near the top of any list when it comes to urban beauty. Functionally though, all of it has essentially vanished, as our myopic heart is intent on only one thing: Must. Get. Through. Traffic.

"Getting through"—whether its traffic, or meetings, or cancer, or another day at the job that's now become eighteen years old—is exactly the wrong mindset. It's what gives endurance a bad name. The reality is that, ranging from the mundane to the truly horrible, there's stuff that happens. These things create pain in our lives, and we must rise to the moment of doing the hard thing, or waiting, or breathing deeply as we face the challenge, or simply just showing up yet again for the three-thousand-fifty-first time because that's what you do.

What you don't do—or at least don't want to do—is to simply check out and wait for it to be over. It's 9:15 in the morning and you're already thinking about getting off work, battling the commute, and pouring a drink. That's a problem, for lots of reasons.

The better way is to take our cue from the hikers who have attuned their senses to see the beauty that's blaring so loudly, or whispering so softly, all around them. This simply requires cultivating gratitude and the capacity to pay attention.

I'm sitting in a meeting as a person is talking on and on about a detail which, though important to him, is of no consequence to me. I'm hungry; tired, too. I've been at work for eleven hours already, and this person's conversation, every second of it, is delaying my release.

I'm listening still, but his thoughts are forming slowly, and there's too much room in my brain. Post sabbatical though, instead of seething, I do two things. First, I take a cookie from a tray on the table we're sitting around and taste it. It was made by a woman with two small children, a lady who has invested time to make this meeting better by adding a touch of beautiful food. I taste the cookie, paying attention especially to the way the chocolate offers a joy to my taste buds by virtue of a perfect cocktail of butter, eggs, just enough sugar, and flour. When the chocolate is crushed by the teeth, it pours forth and blends with everything else, and there's deep pleasure in this, though we don't notice it often enough. I say a prayer of thanks for her and her family, while still seeking to be present.

Second, I look at the person to her left, a staff member who puts in long hours every single day aligning the details of my very complex work so that I can be free to do the very thing I'm doing right now as I write. Again, I'm overwhelmed with gratitude and say a prayer. I'm on a roll now, and soon, my spirit is soaring with gratitude for my job, for these people, and, yes, for this very meeting.

Then I'm fully back. I just needed a minute of paying attention to the beauty of the moment and being grateful. Because of it, I'm restored. Thus is the house of endurance built.

Rest

August 18. *We've been hiking all day in pursuit of our destination in Linderhof. At one point, several kilometers before our arrival, we come to a crossroads: Linderhof to the left, and Graswang, a town unknown to us, to the right. We choose our intended destination, but it's nearly two hours before we arrive in Linderhof. Once there, we make the sad discovery that our reservation, though "in the region of Linderhof," is actually in Graswang. We speak with a local road crew, and they tell us that the address is actually in Graswang. "Don't worry, though," they say. "It's close. Only six kilometers!" My wife, beyond spent at this point, bursts into tears. She'd been rationing physical and emotional energy for the past 10km, intent on being completely spent by the arrival. Now we've arrived, but we aren't there yet. Thankfully, a local bus is available to take us to our destination, and soon we're settled in at a warm guesthouse, just as the rains begin.*

August 20. *It's morning, and we've had a full day's rest in Graswang. We're pondering our next move. As we consider hiking to Oberammergau, we see that it's six kilometers, and my wife says, "Only six? Let's go now!" What was insurmountable less than forty-eight hours earlier is now seen as not only doable, but nothing more than an enjoyable stroll. Oh, the difference a day makes—a day of rest!*

Once again, I appeal to my alpine training manual for guidance, where I learn, "The most underestimated component of a training plan is the recovery." If it's true in training for a race or a mountain peak, it's all the more true in the rest of life. The demands of work, desires of the heart, and personal sense of fear and inadequacy all conspire to keep us "on" incessantly. The wear and tear in such settings happen in all areas of life, body, soul, and spirit. We've all been there. We all know it.

In spite of what we know, the keeping of the Sabbath seems to be the one commandment out of God's big Ten that we break regularly and don't feel a tinge of guilt. It's as if murder, adultery, and theft are, among the Ten, the big three—worthy of censure and church discipline, if not criminal prosecution. This in spite of the fact that those three commands receive a total of one verse each, while Sabbath-keeping is deemed important enough to receive four verses all by itself, offering not just rationale, but an inclusivity for Sabbath rest that extends to visitors, servants, even animals. Everyone, it seems, needs rest.

And yet, rest is the one thing conspicuously absent from most lives in the developed world, even more so at times among the busy nonprofit sector—people who are working so very hard to save the world in various ways. Maybe we should start taking the commandment God spent the most time talking about a bit more seriously, recognizing that we're called to serve our world out of a full cup, and that one of the means whereby our cups are kept full is by learning to practice the discipline of rest.

Faith, gratitude, presence, and rest. Stripped of the burdens of life that steal our joy on a regular basis, we found ourselves settling into a rhythm which provided for restoration. As we'd hoist our packs each morning for another day, more often than not we had a sense of anticipation, and the reason was because of rest, most often found in the river valley towns between journeys in the high country.

Note
[1]Photos for this chapter: http://bit.ly/Endurance11.

TOWNS

A trip provides food for the mind. It helps pull men out of the mire and pollution of old corrupt customs. . . . It accelerates the match of peace and virtue and love.
—Thomas Cook

A man on foot, on horseback, or on a bicycle will see more, feel more, enjoy more in one mile than the motorized tourists can in a hundred miles.
—Edward Abbey

August 24. Ostlerhütte.[1] *I'm awake in the early morning dark at the Ostlerhütte, grateful that the rain and wind have stopped, or at least the silence leads me to believe such. All night we were shaken awake by relentless gales blowing the window open in the middle of the night. One of us would rise and shut it, only to have it blown open again moments later. But now, just before first light, it's blissfully silent. As the room begins its imperceptible brightening, I get out from under the covers to go look out the window, where I discover that the reason for the silence is because the decibels of rain have given way to the quiet of snow.*

This news leads to a new course for us. We decide to forego our planned hike to Bad Kissinger Hütte. Getting there is a steep and rocky path which will be slippery at best, or perhaps buried enough under snow that we might even lose our way. Visibility is poor. Snow is falling. Wind is strong. It's time to go down the mountain.

Ostlerhütte sits on the northern edge of the Alps and, when we arrived earlier, provided stunning views into the flatlands of Germany. The evening we arrived we sat on rocks enjoying the sun setting in the west, watching shadows fall over lush fields. Harvest time is coming already here for some crops, so the land cries ripeness, abundance, and peace.

Those of us who were born after the two World Wars may find it easy to forget that the majestic German alpine areas got ravaged by two of humanity's worst wars. It wasn't always so, of course. This is the land of war, and Reich, of Hitler and genocide, and this dark past isn't hidden away in a corner. The signs of it are in war memorials in nearly every town, in museums and places like Dachau, and in churches, where the names of the dead who died in the wars are written. In the tiny town of Graswang, there's a memorial in the church where these names appear, likely all from one family:

A. Buchwiezer 1918–1944

S. Buchwiezer 1921–1941

G. Buchwiezer 1924–1945

My wife saw a similar memorial in the tiny region of Rohrmoos-Obertal, Austria, where these names were similarly inscribed on their war memorial amidst dozens of others:

Gottlieb Stocker 1906–1945

Johann Stocker 1923–1945

Johann Stocker 1918–1941

Hermann Stocker 1913–1941

Anton Stocker 1906–1944

Anton Stocker 1925–1944

Franz Stocker 1922–1945

I can't imagine that time and place in any way that makes it real for me, an American baby boomer born a decade after the battles for the soul of Europe ended. Still, the names speak of a time of darkness, violence, spiritual and moral blindness, and unfathomable suffering for wives, daughters, sons, cousins. In my travels through Europe over the decades, I've heard stories about that time and place from students and friends whose parents, grandparents, and uncles fought. Some are stories of courage and resistance, others of complicity and complexity. All are stories of loss, of families torn apart, blood shed, and souls ripped apart.

Scenes from the war and right after have found their way into our lives via archived footage we now access easily. We've watched the American soldiers discovering Dachau, seen the devastation that was Dresden, viewed the horrors and weeping of the German people as they discovered what had been done in their name, seen vestiges of courage and grace. I've been privileged to hear some of these things through direct conversations with WWII survivors. But we can never, never know it as they knew it then. The soil of this land was blood and ash, the heart of its people hollowed out.

The darkness of then, though, makes the light of now all the more remarkable. "Weeping may endure for a night, but joy comes in the morning," is how David put it, pondering the infinite, relentless kindness and mercy of God. Thanks be to God that so very often the end of the story isn't really the end of the story at all but the beginning of a brand new chapter.

August 24. Oberstaufen. *Having skipped our night in the snow covered high country at Bad Kissinger Hütte, we decide to make our way, via train, toward some friends we planned to visit before our final days of trekking. We hike down the mountain as the snow turns to rain, and soon we're sitting on a train heading north and west into the agricultural flatlands of Bavaria and Swabia.*

We leave the train at Oberstaufen. Basking in the sun and warmth of the flatlands, we walk toward the center of town where Hotel am Rathaus looks appealing. Making our way inside, we're met by Rolf Schmidt, the proprietor. He's gray, perhaps seventy, with bright eyes and an inviting smile. After a few minutes of conversation, his hospitality and kindness melt us. We can't say no, and so within the hour, we've settled into our room, showered, and are ready to explore the town.

Though the shops are closed, as they always are on Sundays, the piazza is alive with some sort of celebration. There's a "bouncy house" for children, various craft booths, and a small German band playing mostly beer hall music with a few American classics tossed in the mix. We enjoy an outdoor meal, and then a moment unfolds that will forever be seared in my memory.

In a piazza filled with food, fun, and families, the band's closing song for the festival begins and its Louie Armstrong's "A Wonderful World." By now we're walking toward the bandstand, and when the soloist begins articulating what he sees, in English, I realize that he's not just singing a song, he's articulating a reality.

"I see trees of green, red roses too. I see them bloom, for me and you." Yes. This very piazza is overflowing with the life and color that is late summer anywhere in the world where there's water, and peace, and enough resources for flower gardens as a sign of grace and peace. I'm mindful that the words are true words in this exact moment, not aspirational, but descriptive.

"The colors of the rainbow, so pretty in the sky, are also in the faces of people going by. I see friends shaking hands, saying, 'How do you do?' They're really saying, 'I love you.'" As he sings, I see two Muslim women wearing traditional hijab walking together. Over there is a disabled man in a wheelchair with his caregiver. There are different faces, different stories, different cultures, different abilities. The colors of the rainbow in the faces of people going by, in real time, while someone is singing Armstrong's song. Beautiful.

I ponder what it must have been like in this very space when Aryan supremacy was peddled as truth, when fear and hate became the ammunition directed at the other who was different, when the disabled were swept away. Though I can't imagine it fully, I know enough to understand that this place—here—now—is not just beautiful. Its beauty is exponential because of what it displaced.

We walk through town a bit more and randomly come across a poster inviting the public to an organ concert in a tiny church about 3km outside the city. We make our way there in the early evening, as the concert is set for 7:30. The walk takes us through forest and pasture land with spectacular views of the surrounding hills. We arrive early and sit outside in a sort of garden space belonging to the church. In the next thirty minutes, people file into the church and take their places, ready to listen to Bach. The concert begins, and soon everyone is lost in the beauty of the music. "Jesu, Joy of Man's Desiring" wafts through the tiny chapel, and tears come to my eyes as I look at the faces of elderly Germans all around me, Germans old enough to remember. If the word "shalom" embodies not just the absence of war, but the presence of all that is right with the world, this moment has captured it. The light on the hillside as the sun dips lower, the predominately elderly local Germans gathering in their proper traditional clothing, the beauty of the blossoms in the carefully cared for garden. All of it cries perfection, as if changing a single thing about the moment would steal the peace.

As the locals, totaling maybe fifty, pour into the tiny chapel with its pipe organ, I think to myself, "These people have stories to tell—of war and loss, of pain and betrayal,

> *of courage and sacrifice." Now, though, in this moment, it's*
> *just a small pipe organ and some Bach, played artfully on*
> *a Sunday evening as the sun drops in the west, and those*
> *who've seen and heard so much, listen quietly.*
>
> *Shalom. Sorrow in the night, but joy in the morning.*
> *Make it thus, Lord; make it thus.*

Our times in the towns of Germany and Austria afforded us the opportunity to learn about the history of this soil which has known so much war and subsequently such a good measure of peace. This geography and its history stand as a testimony to the good things that can come out of loss and challenge. *Wirtschaftswunder*[2] is the German word for "economic miracle," and it is a term used to describe the rapid economic development of Austria and Germany after the ravages of WWII had destroyed the region. The rebuilding of these two nations required sacrifice, frugality, humility, discipline, and a willingness to compromise and work together for the common good—qualities that are increasingly rare among the prosperous of this world.

They had no choice. Devastation and undeniable loss demanded the best of them. The "economic miracle" created a culture that values caring for "the least of these," which is no surprise since the German leadership after the war came from a devout Catholic named Konrad Adenauer of the Christian Democratic Party. Bringing Protestants and Catholics together in pursuit of a new and better Germany, Adenaur's leadership moved the country from adversity to prosperity with astonishing speed.

On May 18, 1980, there was an explosion and 5.2 magnitude earthquake as Mt. St. Helens in Washington State blew its top. Groves of centuries-old trees were wiped out in a matter of minutes, and Spirit Lake, a popular tourist destination among Washingtonians disappeared under a pile of ash and avalanche debris. The entire area looked like a war zone overnight, and the prospect of ecological recovery seemed dim, at least to the naked eye. One of the first ecologists to arrive on the scene said that it looked as if everything had been utterly destroyed, as if no life would ever spontaneously reappear.

Over thirty-five years later, all is well, in fact better than well. It began with the reappearance of latent moss and brambles, and continued, species after species, until something new had arisen out of the ashes of the old, indeed precisely because of the ashes of the old!

This is the way of it, I now see, with nations like Germany, Austria, and Rwanda, where outbreaks of darkness wrought undeniable devastation, like a volcanic eruption, only worse because of the countless lives lost and hearts broken. The loss became the soil in which real hope was born.

The same thing happens in the lives of individuals. A man gets cancer, and this terrifying event leads to pursuit of eternal things. He shows up at a church service and discovers a hope and meaning he'd never considered before, as he yokes his life with Christ's and begins a new adventure. He starts a foundation to raise money for a cure of the very cancer that visited him. He serves others as never before. Like Scrooge on Christmas day, the man's been reborn, finally finding the life he was created for, but only because the cancer shook him awake.

The Bible is filled with this kind of stuff, only with a twist. The stories I've shared so far in this chapter haven't been told completely. I began by recalling losses, explosions, cancer. In every case, though, a more accurate portrayal would be that before there was loss, there was hope and beauty too—at least in some measure, somehow. It seems that the darkness needn't be the end of the story.

This plot is common in the Bible. God visits Abraham and tells him he'll be a father, and then he waits, and doubts, and waits some more, and sleeps with the maid, which creates all kinds of twisted internal family dynamics when she gives birth to a son. And then Abraham waits some more, and then he argues with God, and laughs, and doubts, gets circumcised, and begs God to let the child born by his maid be enough, and then Isaac, son of Sarah his wife, is born. All the waiting, all the pain, all the failure, is swept away in the renewal of a promise fulfilled.

David is anointed as king, but instead of a dozen inaugural balls to attend, the existing king has it in for him, so he tries to execute him—twice. As a result, David's on the run, hiding in caves, building fake alliances with enemies, feigning insanity, all the while biding his time until "the Lord's anointed" dies and David can claim the throne, which he ultimately does.

Peter enjoys a glorious vision with Jesus on the Mount of Transfiguration, and then there's Jesus's arrest and Peter's denial of ever having known him. His eyes meet Jesus, and he runs out weeping and ashamed. Joseph? After he shares his dreams of greatness with his brothers, they hate him, and he's sold as a slave, framed for rape, tossed in prison, and forgotten. Only after he hits bottom is there a quick turn of circumstance and he's raised up to second in command of the land, used by God to save the lives of the very brothers who hated him and sold him into servitude. A son takes his inheritance from his loving father without a shred of gratitude and quickly squanders it by buying sex and living like hell. Then, broke and ashamed, he returns to find, not a severe chastening, but a party in his honor. The chastening happened all by itself. What was needed for real transformation was for him to know the love of the father, but it was a love that perhaps would never be known apart from his wanderings.

The pattern happens repeatedly in order to show us that this is the way of it: Vision. Dissonance. Failure. Loss. Restoration. It happens so often in the Bible that it's almost axiomatic. There's no light without darkness, no joy without sorrow, no resurrection without crucifixion. In order for God to be known as provider, I need to be in want. I know God as healer when I'm sick, know God as deliverer when I'm stuck in some sort of prison, whether that means a personal addiction or a circumstance I'd never have chosen. I'm stuck in it, at work, at home, in a venture of some sort. It's messy.

Oberstaufen bathed my soul in light. So now I need to tell you that we arrived there accidentally. Our intent all along had been to visit some friends in southern Germany after we'd finished about two-thirds of our trekking adventure. As a result, the snows at Ostlerhütte led to a decision to head west to visit our friends. We boarded a train toward the city of Lindau, intending to spend the night there, and on the train, debated whether this city was on a peninsula of sorts or was an actual island in the large lake Bodensee. Our train compartment companions were listening and chimed in because they actually lived in Lindau. They told us it was, in fact, an island, and advised that it was "more expensive" than other equally lovely places.

They suggested we disembark at Oberstdorf, which they believed was the next stop. We quickly hoisted our packs on our backs and got off, making our way to the center of town by looking at a map near the train station. Having spent a lovely afternoon and evening at a piazza celebration and organ concert, we hiked up a hill the next morning and discovered, looking at a map, that we weren't in Oberstdorf at all, but Oberstaufen!

Looking back on our day there, I'm convinced that we stumbled into that space of Louie Armstrong and J. S. Bach because I needed to learn, once again, what matters most about my faith. We are living in a time when it seems that every once-trusted institution is collapsing. People are cynical about the church due its irrelevance, greed, and hypocrisy. They're cynical regarding government because those we've given power to seem intent only on keeping power, rather than serving and leading.

We're seeing that far too often, black lives don't matter. Police lives don't matter. Lives in the womb don't matter. The lives of single mothers who are alone due to domestic violence don't matter. Lives of those caught in a web of human trafficking and slavery don't matter. Lives of refugees don't matter, or people living on the margins of our prosperous culture. Sometimes we're not sure whether even our own lives matter! It's darkness all around. The cynical among us consider this to be evidence that God is dead. "How could a loving God allow Syria, ISIS, Boko Haram?" they ask, which might well lead to the superficial conclusion that God is absent, or wicked, or, at the very least, weak.

Before we put the nails in the coffin of deity, we'd do well to consider the rest of the story. There's a Hitler, but there's an Adenauer and a *Wirtschaftswunder,* and disabled children playing in the piazza where once they would have disappeared. There's the discovery that a husband has a horrific addiction, but courageous truth-telling and the hard work of restoration lead to a life that's richer and freer than ever before. There's cancer, and there are the stories of radical life reorientation in the wake of that diagnosis, so that lives move forward with heretofore-absent joy, hope, meaning, and calling. And whether their lives are extended for an extra month, or their cancer disappears entirely, the point is that they recovered real life.

A disturbing movement that's afoot in our world is our lust for control, for safety, for protection. When bad things happen, we wonder what we did wrong. "Who sinned?" we want to know, that this death, this war, this disease, this financial collapse happened. Inherent in the question is the false belief that we've cut a bargain with God. We'll give God a little bit of time and money, and keep away from the big sins, and God in exchange will give us parking places downtown, national security, low inflation, and protection from any and all forms of disruption.

We start to believe it sometimes, and when we do, we begin to live as the worst of all people because we begin to be religious, as if we've cut a deal with God. We're the older brother in the story of the Prodigal Son, always doing the right thing in hope that Dad will pay us well. When that's our thinking, it has nothing to do with love and everything to do with greed and fear. To the extent that this becomes the paradigm, we're always living under the twin-sister shadows of shame and pride. When things go wrong, we presume it's us. "What have I done to deserve this?" we ask, and if we and our friends can't think of anything, then we curse God and walk away. Or, perhaps worse, we enjoy success and presume that because business is good and our cholesterol is below two hundred, God's pleased with our priorities and lifestyle. Nothing validates wisdom in the West like wealth and success, and suddenly people want to hear what you have to say, just because your life is good. This too is a waste, for too many reasons to name here. The main reason, though, is that success only proves success; it doesn't imply wisdom.

While listening to Bach in that little chapel and pondering the course of my life, I realize how easily I become one of the proud ones. I'm seeing, too, how pride creates a sort of fear and greed, because now that we have a reputation for success, we'd better keep it or we'll have nothing. Why, when I didn't have success, did I not care about it? Why, now that I have it, am I so afraid to lose it?

The good and bad happen in the world—to everyone. The profundity of the gospel isn't that immunity is granted to the good people. Rather, it lies in the fact that God brings glorious, life-giving transformation right out of the ashes of what should have been catastrophic failure and defeat. People who follow Christ should, of all the people in the world, live most fearlessly. This is because we know that no ashes, no mutant cell, no addiction, no terrorist shooting, no financial downturn, no national crisis, no war, no act of terror is ever the end of the story. Rather, these things become the soil out of which a new and profound life grows.

I sit in the concert listening to Bach's "Jesu."

Jesu, joy of man's desiring
Holy Wisdom, love most bright.

Yes. The holy wisdom of the gospel is that glorious transformation rises out of the ashes, out of the war defeat, out of the genocide, out of the murder. And all of it happens because One rose out of a tomb. I pray:

O Lord God,
I bring my fears of the future to you, mindful that they've
been growing in me,
Mindful that as they've grown, my heart has been
shrinking.
Thank you for this place, this music, this truth,
The holy wisdom that there is nothing irredeemable for the
One who says,
"Behold, I make all things new."
Send me back to my calling deeply rooted in this
confidence,
this hope,
this peace.
Amen.

The sun has set as we exit the chapel and walk back to Oberstaufen in silence, the light of the day all but faded, as we head back to our room, inhaling the fragrant scent of life in a place that once knew extensive death. Thanks be to God.

Notes

[1] Photos for this chapter: http://bit.ly/Towns12.
[2] https://en.wikipedia.org/wiki/Wirtschaftswunder.

LAST TOUR

CHAPTER THIRTEEN

Not all those who wander are lost.

—Bilbo Baggins

Then I heard the voice of the Lord, saying, "Whom shall I send, and who will go for Us?" Then I said, "Here am I. Send me!"

—Isaiah 6:8

It may be that the satisfaction I need depends on my going away, so that when I've gone and come back, I'll find it at home.

Rumi

After weeks of trekking across majestic terrain we had never seen before, we are a bit taken aback by the blessings we experience as familiar scenes on our final trek awaken memories so precious to our souls.[1]

September 18. Dachstein Alps. *After seeing our friends from Seattle off at the train station, we head up to Ramsau, a delightful little village where we have some deep roots by this time in our lives.[2] It's appropriate that these Dachstein Alps will be the stage for our final trek together before Donna heads back to Seattle. After weeks of weather characterized by more clouds than sun, more rain than dry, the second half of September is predicted to be mostly sunny and clear, a glorious finale to summer.*

We leave the trailhead early for this thousand-meter elevation-gain hike. These six kilometers will be the only ones of our four hundred-plus kilometers that we've been on before, a few years ago. I think about how easy it was, with every other step of our trip, to be wide-eyed with wonder simply because it was all new. But now, here, there's an instant sense of déjà vu familiarity. Ah, yes, I remember this little farm that sells fresh buttermilk just before the road turns into a trail. Yes, there's the equipment "bahn," the ski lift that hauls food and material up to the hut because it's impossible to drive there, the view up into a bowl of boulders

*strewn on a bed of lush green and high mountain pine, the
view back to Ramsau, where four years ago we celebrated
Christmas with Hans Peter and his family and watched a
world ski jumping competition. Ramsau, where for years
I've visited a farm run by two women, and shared coffee, life,
laughter, and prayers.*

*We ascend higher still, amazed at the ease with which
we're able to move up, aware that our bodies have been toned
by all the previous journeys so that we now have plenty of
strength for this last ascent. Up. Up. Only up. I look back
again, now higher, and see beyond Ramsau to Schladming,
the town where I've come for twenty years to share life with
the staff and marvelous students from all over the world at
a small Bible school. Donna stops to take some pictures, and
this gives me a chance to bask in the sunlight of this perfect
day, looking down toward places that aren't just names on
a map to me but are life itself, physical markers of a million
memories. I feel like Ebenezer, holding the hand of the ghost
of Christmas past. There I am at the ski jump with Gertraud
one fall, and then a decade later at that same jump with all
my kids one winter day during a world class competition.*

*There's the rock where Hans Peter and I were one
December afternoon because there was no snow yet, so
we hiked instead. We spoke of our shared love of Christ
as companion, of challenges thrown to our ministries by
ever-changing culture, of sport, of our sons, and of our marriages. God. I miss him. There's the Hochwurzenhütte, where
Hans Peter and I skied up, along with our wives, to dine on
schnitzel and strudel, and linger over the food with laughter
and conversation too long. We left the restaurant, stepping
out into a dark night filled with snow, as we skied down*

*an unlit path back to the car. There's the church where I sat
with the pastor and learned the history of the area—how
Protestants and Catholics fought and eventually reconciled,
how Bible studies were held in cold barns tucked away in
high alpine valleys to avoid persecution, stories of fear and
courage, of persecution and reconciliation. This geography
is my home away from home, and the high vantage allows a
view of the whole past.*

*We arrive at (isn't the name somehow appropriate, in
light of this sabbatical?) the Güttenberghaus by early afternoon and enjoy a bit of soup before going to our room for
a rest. The days are rapidly getting shorter, so when we ask
our host about the possibility of a late day-hike to the top of
Scheichenspitz, he tells us it will take too long, tells us that
we should head over to the summit of Sinabell instead. There
are maybe ninety minutes of sunlight left, a bit longer 'til it's
dark, but I want to share one last moment on a summit with
my wife before she heads home.*

*We navigate the path from the hut down a bit then
up over a pass which takes us into a different world. The
south-facing view is of the lush farmland of Ramsau and
the Enns River valley, with Schladming and lights and clear
cuts for ski runs that double as pasture land in the summer.
I "know" this valley, love this valley. To the north, though, is
the wild side—treeless, endless views beyond glacially formed
canyons in the Styrian Dachstein all the way into upper
Austria. These are places I've never been. The distant mountains turn pink as the sun fades. Step by step, we make our
way upward in silence, as if we're in a cathedral or temple
of some sort, maybe because we are—as if this moment is
utterly holy, maybe because it is.*

"These sides represent potential futures," I say to myself. To my right, the known, familiar, secure. To my left, uncharted territory awaiting exploration but full of uncertainty. We're always choosing, aren't we? Will we stay on the familiar path or step toward the unknown? The right answer depends on God's guidance in our lives, because there is, after all, a time for everything, including times to stay or go. Sometimes we stay out of fear when we should actually go. Other times we leave too soon, out of frustration or boredom, when it's actually time to stay. The staying or going isn't the question. "Do I believe that God cares about such things, and am I listening for God's voice and responding in obedience?" That is the real question.

Jesus tells us that we need faith "like little children." Theologians, ironically, pontificate and debate what that means, delving into lexical studies and exegetical nuances to understand first-century children, but, of course, there's a debate about who actually wrote the various Gospels, so that becomes a debate too, along with the lexical meaning and nuances of the word "children." I don't like these theological rabbit holes because truth is usually not that complicated. How about, instead of debating what Jesus meant, or who recorded what he said, we spend time looking at children. If we do this, we'll find that all children share two things in common: vulnerability, and a willingness and desire to receive from others, especially their parents.

We learned it early at our mother's breast, and later on our dad's shoulders, if we were fortunate. When we skinned our knee, we ran to one of them, and also when we were scared. Alone? They were companionship. Confused? They were wisdom. Cold? They wrapped us in their overcoat at the football game to keep us warm. To the extent that we grew up in a healthy family, we always went to them and never wondered if we'd be welcome, or if we'd need to pay our way.

Things change, though, as we grow into adulthood, because we become the producers, and we take on roles as providers, caregivers, leaders, and creators. In the midst of all that production, childlike faith leaks away and we adopt a different mindset. We begin defining ourselves and our significance by our production, reputation, or net worth. It's our attempt, in my opinion, to cover our nakedness with a fig leaf. "Look at me! I'm wealthy. I started a business. I lead a great big church. I wrote five books. I ran a marathon. I raised great kids who love Jesus." Whatever.

It's like climbing without a rope, though, because when the day comes that we can no longer produce, when our fig leaves crumble and drop off, we'll find ourselves naked and ashamed, wondering what we're worth. At my age, I'm wondering, "What will I be worth when I'm not the senior leader of a big thing, when the phone stops ringing, when big decisions are being made by other people instead of me? What then? Who will I be?" These thoughts have haunted me off and on throughout my sabbatical. The future, eventually, brings change, and some of those changes will be hard.

With every upward step toward the summit, the beauty of these moments in this place, unmatched by anything we've experienced in our previous forty days, drowns out all my anxieties. Light becomes muted imperceptibly, but inevitably, as we ascend. Silence baptizes everything like a symphony. It's as if God is pouring all the perfection of the universe into this little piece of the Alps. God's Presence is more than real, if that's possible, as everything comes together for us in a moment of complete shalom. Our bodies are at their peak strength. The trip has so intertwined our lives as husband and wife that our marriage is closer to one than it's ever been, a "one" now seasoned by adaptations, arguments, revelations, confessions, aging. Our love of mountain beauty and our longing to be part of it is met by God on this particular evening with a resounding "Yes!" as if God pours the perfect cocktail of light, shadow, color, majesty, and silence into the sky and soil of these Alps for these few moments, saying, "Here. Just for you. Bon Appetite." It's the kind of overpowering beauty that invites worship and makes me believe in thin places.[3]

As we ascend the ridge, the summit of this very minor peak comes into view, and I'm surprised to see a cross. Unlike any we've seen on summits thus far, this one's small, humble, rustic. Without words, we know what will happen. Donna goes first, sitting next to the cross as she opens the metal box that is the summit registry and begins to write, while I wait. It's her moment at the cross, in a silent world baptized in pure infinite beauty, from the heights of the darkening sky to the last of the summer wildflowers at our feet.

After a time, I approach and we're together at the cross, looking down on this little part of the world that has become so precious to us. There are tears, overflowing from deep joy and gratitude for this gift of this time we've been given and for this perfect climax. We pray together, and then it's my turn to be alone at the cross.

In the summit book, I write a word of gratitude to the Creator for the gift of places like this, for the gift of strength and time to be in this very place at this very moment, and then I stop writing and this outpouring of gratitude becomes a wordless prayer. I know that this perfect moment won't last. We'll descend back to the hut, and then tomorrow, down to the valley, and then in a few weeks, I'll hop on a jet and all this perfection, this shalom, this contentment, will fade away.

More significant, though, is the realization that the world I'm returning to is changing. My kids have left home, so my role as a dad is changing. And with respect to my work, as sure as the sun goes down, the day is coming, whether its two years from now or ten, when I'll hand things off there too; and then . . . what? These thoughts erupt while I'm at the cross, where I decide, "What better time to pour out my heart to my Creator than at the cross." So I do, in words, tears, questions.

When I began this journey weeks ago, my relationship with God had become "tired," like someone who's been walking too long without a rest. Things that once had meaning had hardened into little more than rituals. Weariness and words had often displaced passionate longings and outpourings, whether of joy or sorrow. Today, though, all that perfunctory religion is gone, displaced by a sense that the God I once knew well and loved passionately is here—intensely present—as I pray. I can hear God's voice in response to my outpourings:

"I'm enough," God says to me, not audibly, but in a flood of recognition that I've been privileged to participate in a story of hope that God is writing in the world, and that the participation has been overwhelmingly a joy. God has always been enough. My calling has been punctuated by a balanced rhythm of leading a local church and all its continuity, and of teaching in various places across the globe, with all the learning and joy that come from that. I want to freeze this pattern and calling in my life and keep it forever.

This longing, though, betrays the reality that while I may sing about God's being enough, it's really God plus the blessings of my job, and health, reputation, and travel that are enough. And now, as I look to a horizon where these things will inevitably change, I worry that I won't be as much, and I'm afraid. Afraid of insignificance, afraid nobody will call. These fears rise up right in the midst of this beauty because this alpine perfection fading into darkness is metaphor to me, even as I stand here. It's a picture of how life teases you with gifts and then snatches them away. You arrived empty-handed, you'll leave that way too. The Bible even says this.

When my body's old, my job's gone, my kids are too busy for me, will God really be enough?

All this is swirling in my head when I hear three exhortations from God: **"I *was* enough—remember?"** There in the Alps, I remember the moment when I believed, with all my heart, that knowing God was enough.

February 1976. Sierra Nevada Mountains. *I'm a single college guy at a ski retreat, chasing a blonde and excited to get away from my architecture studies for a weekend. On Saturday night, I'm one of maybe one hundred fifty students who've all piled into a little chapel so that we might hear Earl talk to us out of Jeremiah 9:23–27, which is this passage about how knowing God is the highest pursuit we can have in our lives and how all of us need to make it our supreme priority. Earl's old, but looks wizened, and I can't stop listening to him. He's some distance into his talk when he stops, points right at me, and says, "For some of you there are other things you're pursuing more than God—career goals, sexual pleasure, financial security. You like God, but God's second or third." Then he looks around the room, but I feel as if he's looking at me only, speaking to me only, when he says, "You're robbing yourself of the life God created you for if you don't make knowing God your highest pursuit. God. Is. Enough."*

I am pierced by this moment in the mountains, and it changes my life forever. I step out into the forest after the meeting and kneel down in the snow. What he said resonated deeply with me because, in spite of my fierce pursuits of architecture, my desire to make a mark in the world, my social life at college, at the core I'm lonely, depressed, and clueless regarding what will constitute a meaningful future. Much of this is because I miss my dad desperately. Now, I've been offered the hope that there's someone who is, as the bearded man said, "a Father to fatherless," and I weep,

> *knowing I want to know this Father because I have no*
> *other. So I pray something like, "God, I don't know what this*
> *means, but I know this much: I want to make knowing you*
> *the number one priority in my life, my main thing. Show me*
> *how to do this, I pray. Amen."*

"I *am* enough. Rejoice!" I'm stricken, in that powerful word, with realization that far too often I fail to live my life on the path of gratitude that enjoys the "enough" of God in the present, so occupied am I with what's around the corner. I was this way more than once in the Alps; so eager to see what's coming over the ridge that I'd rush there, forsaking the beauty of the moment. Why!? I am worrying about tomorrow, when right here, right now, I'm enjoying health, intimacy, abundance, and the beauty of these mountains I love. All of it gets stolen by fear and worry, and this doesn't just happen on mountaintops. It happens every day of our lives as we rush past sunrises, or the beauty of our spouse combing her hair in the morning, or our children wanting to play, or the smell of the wood smoke from the campfire, or that little bit from Bach coming out of the elevator. All the potential moments of worship and gratitude are stolen, sacrificed on the altar of anxiety.

No more. I look around and pour out praise and gratitude for all this beauty and the vast privilege of being here, now. God *is* enough! The dawning realization brings tears to my eyes again, and again I say, "Thank you."

To which God replies one last time, **"I will be enough. Continue!"**

There's a mountain across the valley when I look south. It's a place for the nations, because the World Cup of Skiing was here just a few years ago. I think about God's future for this beautiful broken planet, because it too is centered on a mountain for the nations:

Now it will come about that
In the last days
The mountain of the house of the LORD
Will be established as the chief of the mountains,
And will be raised above the hills;
And all the nations will stream to it.
And many peoples will come and say,
"Come, let us go up to the mountain of the LORD,
To the house of the God of Jacob;
That He may teach us concerning His ways
And that we may walk in His paths."
For the law will go forth from Zion
And the word of the LORD from Jerusalem.
And He will judge between the nations,
And will render decisions for many peoples;
And they will hammer their swords into plowshares and
    their spears into pruning hooks.
Nation will not lift up sword against nation,
And never again will they learn war. (Isa. 2:2–4)

I try to imagine this mountain, or any mountain, circled by nations joining hands and ascending, not in competition with one another for a two-week celebration like the Olympics, but because justice has come to all nations, all peoples, and as a result war has ended, and, of course, terror too. The environment, raped and ravaged by economic greed, has been restored. All that was lost has been found; all that was sick has been healed.

I can't see it. Peace? Justice? Healing? Abundance? Reconciliation? Nothing challenges my faith more, because what I see in this world are race riots in America, mutant viruses spreading across the planet, and ground waters disappearing due to drought or being polluted by mining and drilling practices. I see human trafficking and racism. Fringe groups are dealing in terror, beheading children and cab drivers, raping women and using them as prizes in the spoils of war. It appears as if hell is winning nearly everywhere I turn. No, sometimes I really can't imagine it.

And then I can. I can because I've seen dozens of WWII memorials during these forty days, reminders that this geography so presently saturated with peace and beauty wasn't always so. We've spent these days in blood-stained hills and valleys, in homes and huts that, "if these walls could talk," would have stories of horror to tell that would steal your peace and give you nightmares.

Now, though? Redemption and restoration have happened. Right there in the piazza in Oberstaufen, and in the countless testimonies of changed lives I encounter every year among the students and guests when I travel, and among the congregation I lead. The colors of hope are everywhere; we just need eyes to see.

So, yes, God. I believe it. Peace will come. You will reign. Beauty will flower across the deserts of human cultures and nations once again. I don't know why it hasn't happened sooner; I don't know when it will happen; but in this moment, I know this much: You, God, can do this—will do this.

As soon as I say this, it's obvious. If that's the story God is writing, I'll have a role in it. I might be strong in the future, or I might be weak. Rich or poor. Powerful or living alone in the high mountains. The glory of the gospel is that there's a place for everyone in God's story, so the important question isn't "how long can I stay in this place?"—as if I need to hang on to whatever it is I am intent on keeping that strokes my insecure longings for prestige or influence. The important question is, "Do I believe that God will be with me and express life through me until the very end?"

If my answer is yes, then I need to smile and get on with being the presence of hope and leave the money, location, position, and all other details on the table for God to manage. This isn't an apologetic for passivity. I'll still come home to important and difficult decisions that need to be made. It is, though, an apologetic for making those decisions with empty hands, releasing the future utterly to God because I realize that, come what may, God will have a place for me in his story, because there's a place for everyone—young and old, weak and strong, rich and poor, at the top of the org chart or without any spot on an org chart. Everyone has a place at God's table, and this is beautiful.[4]

I open my hands, and because I do, something happens on that mountain that is monumental. In that moment, I'm free. And rejoicing. The shalom of the landscape has now become the shalom of my heart too. And now, I'm ready to go home. Instead, I'll stay, and my wife will go home, because there are lessons yet to learn, lessons that can only be learned alone.

Notes

[1] Photos for this chapter: http://bit.ly/Lasttour13.

[2] I've been teaching at a little Bible School in Austria one week a year for twenty years.

[3] "Thin places" are places where Celtic Christians believe the barrier between the seen and unseen world is highly permeable. Many of these places are mountains.

[4] A video of our last days of hiking together in the Alps can be found at: http://bit.ly/alpstourfinale.

SOLITUDE

It is in solitude that we discover that being is more important than having, and that we are more than the results of our efforts. In solitude we discover that life is not a possession to be defended, but a gift to be shared.

—Henri Nouwen

Let him who cannot be alone beware of community. . . .
Let him who is not in community beware of being alone. . . .
Each by itself has profound perils and pitfalls. One who wants fellowship without solitude plunges into the void of words and feelings, and the one who seeks solitude without fellowship perishes in the abyss of vanity, self-infatuation, and despair.

—Dietrich Bonhoeffer

Whom have I in heaven but You?
And besides You, I desire nothing on earth.

—Psalm 73:25

September 28. Schladming.[1] *The Bible school where I teach in Austria started their fall term five days ago. The needs of the Bible school are why this sabbatical unfolded in Europe in the first place, rather than according to my original plan to hike the Pacific Crest Trail. Because we have children living in Europe, my wife is leaving to visit them. I'll be teaching a bit and writing between now and October 20, which is the day I leave to return to my life in Seattle.*

There's a wedding in Switzerland we are both invited to, but I elect to stay in Austria, so "goodbye" to my wife consists of a quick hug before she gets in the car with friends to drive away for the wedding. She'll be at the wedding and then visit our daughter and son-in-law for a few days before heading home. I'm on my own now. It's time to learn about solitude.

Moses is one of my favorite people in the Bible, because I share a few things with him:

- He was adopted. I'm adopted.
- He was a reluctant leader. I'm a reluctant leader.
- He had a few "Why this, God? Why now? Why me?" encounters with the Divine. So have I.

What's most striking for me about Moses, though, is the degree to which solitude shapes him. He's alone with God when he wrestles with his call, alone with God in his frustrations and fears as a leader, alone with God for forty days on the mountaintop while he receives directives regarding what it means for Israel to be "the people of God." The gift of being able to be alone with God for extended periods of time is surely rare. It has always been rare. Moses, however, not only was able to pull it off, he seemed comfortable there. I wonder why? Though we can't really know, I do believe that those who are adopted often choose to be alone in life, and that while choosing isolation is surely a liability, it is a liability that can be transformed into an asset.

We who are adopted sometimes have a hard time giving ourselves fully to others. We were, after all, "abandoned." One therapist writes,

> The idea that a birthmother loved her baby so much
> that she gave him away makes no sense to a child. The
> equation is love = abandonment. Allowing one's self
> to love and be loved, therefore, may be associated with
> subsequently being abandoned. The baby doesn't care why
> his birthmother gave him up for adoption; the baby just
> feels abandoned. And that abandoned baby lives in each
> and every adoptee all of his or her life.[2]

This can, and does, create a sense of loneliness in adopted children. We often have an over-the-top fear of rejection, and one of the preferred methods of avoiding said rejection is to build good walls. Where there's no relationship, there's no risk of loss. Only retrospectively can I see how profoundly this shaped my early years. Though friendly and popular at school, I was often, by choice, alone outside school hours. We had that basketball hoop over the garage, and though I'd shoot baskets literally for hours on end, it was extremely rare that friends would join me. "No guys live nearby," I'd say, both to myself and my parents, as an excuse for my solitude.

This was true, and as I result I became a decent basketball player. Every day at school there were pick-up basketball games at lunch where we, a bunch of pubescent boys looking for identity, would run up and down the court so intensely that our social studies class, just after lunch, smelled like a gym. But it was, in the end, just a bunch of insecure egos in search of identity. I never saw the games as a platform for building relationships.

This kind of isolation was the default mode through most of middle school and high school, although high school offered a few deeper friendships. Still, I was "on the outside" in my church youth group, through no fault of my peers. Alone felt safe, risk-free. I doubt I'm alone in pursuing the safety of isolation. Nor is this a new problem. C. S. Lewis wrote that "to love at all is to be vulnerable. Love anything and your heart will be wrung and possibly broken. If you want to make sure of keeping it intact, you must give it to no one."[3]

Yes. Been there—done that. That these tendencies, while present with greater frequency among adoptees, are shared in greater or lesser degrees by all of us is something I've learned through my years in pastoral ministry. The bottom line is that all of us are ambivalent about relationships. We want intimacy because we're made for it, and as a result our hearts long for it, deeply. At the same time, we all know the pain of betrayal, rejection, and loss. Getting close to people is like climbing without a rope. The higher you go, the harder you fall. "Better," some of us often think, "to stay closer to the ground—safer, predictable, risk-free." And thus is loneliness born. Isolation rooted in fear will always lead to an ache in our hearts, because the truth of the matter is that we're made for relationships, made for intimacy, both vertically with God and horizontally with other people, and we won't really be able to fully rest if, out of fear, we're cutting ourselves off from people.

This was often my paradigm throughout my childhood and into early adulthood, with one glaring exception: I loved my dad fiercely. Maybe it was because of the story he told me about my adoption. When I was maybe ten years old, my parents sat with me and said, "You know, Richard, in most families, parents end up with the children they have because they're born into their family. But adopted children are different than that in a special way. They're chosen. And, Richard, we chose you!"

I learned this well before I learned about sex and reproduction, so my next logical question was, "Why did you choose me?" I asked my dad, and he told me that when I was six months old, I was one among many in a room full of cribbed babies. Mom and Dad walked past each crib as part of the decision-making process, and Dad said that he held out his thumb and wiggled it in front of each baby. After a few responses ranging from outright rejection to apathy, they came to me, and I reached for the thumb and held on. "And that," said my dad, "was good enough for us."

Only years later would the profound significance of my reaching for his thumb sink in. That motion landed me in a family with a rich Christian heritage, exposing me to a Bible teacher from England when I was about twelve, which would ultimately become a significant part of my calling. More significant in the moment, though, was that hearing the story gave birth to the deepest trust, intimacy, and bonding of any relationship I'd have in my life until marriage.

My dad, busy and health-challenged, made time for me. On Saturdays, I'd go with him to the school office where he was superintendent, and during his breaks he'd hit me fly balls. When he'd come home from work, he'd spend time with me, playing H-O-R-S-E with the basketball. I didn't know then that he couldn't play a little one-on-one because his lungs were compromised due to numerous childhood bouts with pneumonia. Only later did I realize that even playing H-O-R-S-E, a game requiring only shooting rather than movement, was a challenge for him. His investment, I came to discover, was sacrifice—pure love for me, not love for basketball.

On an October Friday night when I was seventeen, I came home from a high school football game where I'd played in the marching band, and my mom told me, "Dad's fallen into a coma, and if you want to see him alive, you'd better go to the hospital now. They don't think he'll make it through night." He didn't.

After the funeral, I sank into a depression, the marks of which were a deep sense of loneliness and insecurity. The one I trusted most, the one I loved most, was gone. I didn't lash out at God, didn't fall into the abyss of an addiction. I just dropped out. Of everything. I decided to pursue architecture so that there'd be some mark of me left on the earth after I died. Heart wounds don't go away though. They became the soil out from which I would begin seeking Christ as my true companion and lifelong friend.

This is often the way of it. Our moves toward God come most profoundly and with the deepest sense of reality in the midst of loss, betrayal, and failure. We are aware of our need for deeper realities when we can't escape our pain, when there's nowhere else to turn. My story includes death and adoption. Other stories include abuse, addiction, infidelity, infertility, war, accidents, and all the rest that makes this world fallen. What an amazing paradox that the most profound losses can become the soil in which the deepest eternal relationship can become real.

October 11, 2014. *I rise early and make my way up toward Güttenberghaus for the final hike of my sabbatical. Having taught a full load of classes the previous week, I've no time for an extended overnight trip. But on this last weekend in Austria, my hope is to reach the summit of Eselstein, which Donna and I had failed to reach a few weeks earlier. It's unquestionably autumn. A thick frosty mist hangs in Enns River valley as I leave before 7 A.M., extending up into the plateau beneath the Dachstein range where I'm headed.*

Not only am I alone while hiking, but this being the end of the season, I'm alone when I arrive at Güttenberghaus. Thick fog gives way to stunning views of the Dachstein Alps, with a dusting of fresh snow frosting the stone faces. Set against the blue sky, the scene is stunning, and I'm amazed that, among the billions in the world, even among the thousands presently in this little valley, there's no one else on this trail just now. At the hut, I enjoy a hot cocoa with a mound of whipped cream on top before pressing on toward Eselstein. The path will take me to a moonscape of rocky terrain, well above tree line.

Because I'm alone, every decision is mine. Take this side trail for a few minutes or continue to my destination? Stop and sit to catch my breath, or press on without a break? Continue to the summit in spite of the fact that there's a slick verglas coating on the steep rocky path as I press higher, or return to the safety of the hut? Every decision is mine, and I am enjoying, every step of the way, a pace that's perfect for me!

". . . a pace that's perfect for me . . ." Yes. This is one of the genuine gifts of moving into the discipline of solitude, a discipline far different than simply being alone, because I've come to discover through thirty-five years of marriage and nearly the same number of years in ministry that the loneliness of my youth was rooted in aversion. Fear of rejection, or conflict, or complexity, led me to adopt a mode of survival in my earlier days that simply said "not worth the hassle," as I'd withdraw from others, never overtly, but in the friendliest of ways.

Solitude, on the other hand, has to do with the capacity to distance ourselves from the prevailing noise of culture and the demands of other people enough that we become responsive to the inner voice of Christ instead, so that we're increasingly shaped by his priorities, not those foisted on us by our world. We grow intimate with God through prayer, reading, and an ever-developing awareness of the Presence of God among us, speaking through creation, circumstances, other people, and inner conviction. The practitioner of solitude also develops a growing awareness of Christ within us, a guiding voice, a source of strength, and an ever-present companion. Solitude enables us to travel to the beat of a different drummer, the result of which is a joy, contentment, and peace that move us ever closer to the life we are created for. Perhaps the most important fruit of this for me is that Christ leads me not to withdrawal, but to hospitality, friendship, service, and deeper relationships. The discipline of solitude has liberated me from isolation and loneliness.

This is ridiculously freeing in another way as well. Solitude moves us from performance approval to the pursuit of our true calling. We live in a culture that dishes out approval or condemnation so powerfully that we are, most of us, driven by the voices of others rather than the voice of God. Henri Nouwen writes about this:

> When we start being too impressed by the results of our work, we slowly come to the erroneous conviction that life is one large scoreboard where someone is listing the points to measure our worth. And before we are fully aware of it, we have sold our soul to the many grade-givers. That means we are not only in the world, but also of the world. Then we become what the world makes us. We are intelligent because someone gives us a high grade. We are helpful because someone says thanks. We are likable because someone likes us. And we are important because someone considers us indispensable. In short, we are worthwhile because we have successes. And the more we allow our accomplishments—the results of our actions— to become the criteria of our self-esteem, the more we are going to walk on our mental and spiritual toes, never sure if we will be able to live up to the expectations which we created by our last successes.[4]

We're at grave risk of being shaped, in other words, by the forces of our cultural narrative rather than by the voice of God. This problem presents itself in a myriad of pathologies, ranging from workaholism to secret addictions, from infidelity to oceans of insecurity among the religiously compliant who have been robbed of the grace found in the true Christ and instead are living under the threat of condemnation dished out by institutional Christianity.

Even if no other voices are calling out to us, we have the voices inside our heads that we must deal with. John calls these inner voices "the lust of the flesh and the lust of the eyes and the boastful pride of life" (1 John 2:16). This unholy trinity of voices shout to us that life is to be found "over here" among virtual pleasures so freely available now, or among endless acquisition of stuff to bolster our reputation, or among success in positioning ourselves above others. The voices are always there and, in our vulnerable moments, are appealing.

All of this—the combined call of the voices of our world and the voices of our own corruption—is a far cry from the "life abundant" Christ came to give us. The way out resides in the discovery of solitude, because solitude withdraws from all the other voices and draws near to God alone. When my motives for decisions are driven by reputation advancement, pain avoidance, pleasure indulgence, wealth creation, or any of myriad other dubious voices rather than by the simple question, "What is the will of God in this moment?" then I'll quickly find myself on the wrong path.

Learning to hear and respond to the voice of God necessitates withdrawal from other voices on a regular basis, and this is the point of solitude. Withdrawal from all the other voices increases our capacity to discern the voice of God. Bolstered by this increased capacity for hearing the voice that matters most, we're able to move back into the whirlwind of daily living, directed from the center, the Spirit, Christ. Herein is peace. Herein is freedom. Herein is life.

As I prepare to head home, I am discovering that these last weeks of sabbatical, without the companionship of my wife, have reminded me of the beautiful foundation of solitude with Christ to which all of us are invited.

I wish, at this point, that I could offer some sort of twelve-step program (or if I were a slick marketer, eleven steps) for enjoying intimacy with God. The problem is that, while there are habits that make for intimacy, something more than habits is required. When a married man seeking to recover a vibrant love for his wife asks her what she needs, she might say, "I need flowers once in a while, and eye contact when I'm talking to you. Oh, and a little help in the kitchen would be nice too." Maybe the worst thing the guy could do at that point would be to set about doing those things in a sort of checklist mentality. "Flowers? Check. Eye contact? Done. Kitchen help? Did the dishes, Honey. Are we in love again yet?"

No. That's because, ultimately, the things we do outwardly should be an expression of the deepest longings of our heart, and unless our heart genuinely wants intimacy with all the vulnerability and nakedness of soul that goes with it, intimacy won't happen, even with flowers and kitchen help. The heart matters more than anything else. What, in the deepest recesses of your being, do you want? Comfort? A good reputation? A successful career or ministry? What does your heart want?

The best practices of solitude have been born out of a broken and lonely heart, broken enough that all the seeker wants—but wants in a desperate way—is friendship with God. My motivation for reading my Bible, for going on walks alone, spending nights out under the stars, journaling . . . all these things are rooted in a genuine longing to know God and enjoy friendship with Christ, longings that were born out of emptiness.

The reason this intimacy is available to all of us is because we're all empty, broken. Under the sheen of respectability that comes with wealth and status lie insecurities, uncertainties, and hidden failures. The challenge doesn't come in being broken or not; the challenge comes in facing it, and at this point, the truth is that the thicker our covering of competencies, the easier it is for us to keep hiding there! This is why Jesus said it was hard for rich people to enter the Kingdom of God. This is why, when he walked on this earth, it was those with nothing to lose who were most receptive and those with the most to lose, humanly speaking, who were resistant.

I'm not grateful my dad died when I was seventeen. I'm grateful that the void created by that terrible loss became the soil in which a longing for intimacy with God could grow. So the real question— the first question—should be, "What's the void in your life, the place of emptiness that, if you faced it courageously, would in your soul fan the spark of longing for God into a full-blown fire?" Start there, friends. Step away from the crowds. Shut off your phone. Listen to the cry of your heart. Let the healing begin.

Notes

[1]Photos for this chapter: http://bit.ly/Solitude14.

[2]Neil Rosentha, "Adoptee's Struggle for Intimacy," *Neil Rosenthal*, June 5, 2006, http://www.neilrosenthal.com/adoptees-struggle-intimacy/.

[3]C. S. Lewis, *The Four Loves*, reissue edition (San Francisco: HarperOne, 2017).

[4]Henri Nouwen, quoted in *Solitude: Seeking Wisdom in Extremes*, by Robert Kull (Novato, California: New World Library, 2008), 203.

AFTERWORD

HOME

CHAPTER FIFTEEN

Peace—that was the other name for home.

—Kathleen Norris

We shall not cease from exploration
And the end of all our exploring
Will be to arrive where we started
And know the place for the first time.

—T. S. Eliot

Come to Me, all who are weary and heavy-laden,
and I will give you rest.

—Jesus the Christ (Matt. 11:28)

Have you seen *The Nutcracker?* Tchaikovsky's marvelous ballet is filled with fantastic encounters for Clara, the young girl whose Christmas Eve gift of a nutcracker is magically transformed into a prince. The prince and Clara are then transported into the "Land of Sweets," ruled by a Sugar Plum Fairy, where they are entertained by various dancers parading past them, until the two of them begin to float away during the finale. As the music reaches a climax, at the very last second, Clara wakes in her bed and realizes it was all a dream.

Coming home from sabbatical felt that way—an abrupt finale whereby the entire experience quickly faded to dream status, and I found myself wondering if it had really happened at all. I arrived back in Seattle to face the reality of some much-needed repairs to our house, which we were intending to sell. Some sewer problems had, shall we say, "spilled" into our home, requiring urgent interior repairs in the basement, not to mention a new sewer line to be laid from the house to the street. We'd decided to move, and our new location required a commute for me several times a week, an experience unknown in my previous twenty years of urban ministry in Seattle. Sitting on the freeway after a full day of work would quickly reveal the worst parts of me. There were moments when I wondered if I'd learned anything at all while away, as I felt my pulse and blood pressure rise in response to the reality that I'm just another one of these multiplied thousands of people with places to go, each of us alone, busy, and in the way of the others.

Work was like jumping into the deep end of a cold pool, as some major decisions had been deferred until my return, intensifying the workload for the first few weeks. I'd learn that two of my three senior leaders would be leaving soon, one due to retirement, the other due to his desires to try out rural living, an opportunity afforded him by the perfect job offer granted to his wife. The loss of these two would mean more change and upheaval in an environment where change was already in abundance, as we'd started five churches in the past five years, creating a scattering of our congregants across the city and changing relational dynamics for them and work dynamics for our staff.

Meetings piled on meetings. The elders gathered to discuss potentially divisive theological matters and funding/permitting issues related to our plans for a new building to replace one that had long outlived its usefulness. Transitions. New hires. Searches. Staff meetings were wrestling with questions about worship capacity on Sundays, change management, staff health, and how to make sure that our now six different locations all continued to represent the core of our identity while also having the freedom to express that identity in localized ways.

Sure enough, the curtain had fallen and just like *The Nutcracker*, it was all a dream. I was back in "production mode" in less time than it took me to overcome jet lag. Life was once again a video game, and I was reacting more than acting. Getting through events, rather than being fully present. "So this is the way of it," I remember thinking to myself by the middle of December. The treadmill that is twenty-first-century living is inescapable.

There were parts of my job I still loved, parts that were life-giving. I began ministry years ago because I loved saturating my heart and mind with the Scriptures and building bridges between what I'm learning and the culture, sharing my discoveries with the people I'm speaking to. Nothing gives me more joy in life, and that I'm granted the opportunity to do this every week is one of life's greatest gifts. I'm also able to teach new young leaders to do the same thing as we gather weekly to study what we'll all be preaching from the next weekend. These responsibilities are precious gifts, and that I'm able to invest in them on a weekly basis is a great privilege. I know that, and I'm grateful.

Still, I'd hoped that I would have come back different—wiser, calmer, with a greater capacity to see the right path forward and follow it. I'd envisioned coming home as a sort of mystic, transformed and wiser for having been on the mountain with God. I've told people that I want to be Gandalf[1] when I grow up, and I'm only half kidding when I say it. I want to be wise and serve others from a heart filled with wisdom.

Instead, life felt very much the same as it had before leaving. What happened?

Two Years Later, November 17, 2016. *There's no power in the cabin where I'm staying up here high in the Sierra Nevada Mountains of California. Heated only by electricity, the cabin is getting colder by the moment as the temperature outside hovers in the twenties. I started the morning wearing only pants and a shirt. Now I've added a vest, slippers, and a ski hat. Soon I'll add a jacket, and I'll need to find a way to sustain power for my computer so I can finish this chapter.*

These are the mountains I'd originally thought would be in my sabbatical journey, the mountains of my childhood. Last night as I hiked on a trail, I grabbed some manzanita leaves and pinched them between my fingers. They released the scent of my youth, and as I put my fingers to my nose, the fragrance released a flood of memories and I was reminded of just how powerfully my life and personality were formed in this Sierra Nevada range.

It was here I met God in a powerful way at camp as a child. It was here that I made my way to Yosemite a few times, hiking up the back side of Half-Dome, soaking in the majesty, finding respite from the heat of the valley, and later falling in love with the woman who would become my wife.

> *It was in these mountains that I prayed under the stars, reorienting my life to make knowing God intimately the main pursuit. That prayer and goal has become my north star, the priority to which I return every time I feel overwhelmed, confused, or weary. All these memories come rushing back as I inhale the scent on my fingers.*

The Scent of Hope

"Thanks be to God, who always leads us in triumph in Christ, and manifests through us the sweet aroma of the knowledge of Him in every place" (2 Cor. 2:14).

Scent and aroma are on my mind as I write because it's thick in the air in these Sierras, so I ponder the audacious claim of Paul the apostle regarding his self-proclaimed "constant state of triumph."

"Come on, Paul. You just finished telling us that you've come through a dark period during which you 'despaired even of life' (2 Cor. 1:8). You're about to catalog your setbacks on the journey that is your ministry, as you recall your experiences of imprisonments, labors, beatings (times without number!!), often in danger of death, shipwrecked, stoned and left for dead (2 Cor. 11:22–25). You remind me of Don Quixote, the man who lives in an alternate universe of his own fabrication. You're denying the realities of your suffering, your setbacks, your sadness. Triumph? If yours is a life of triumph, I'll pass."

My presumption, though, misses the very point that Paul is making. He's saying that conventional notions of triumph must be deconstructed and a truer definition articulated if we're going to enjoy the life for which we're created. Paul's experiences are surely anti-triumph, if triumph is defined as popularity, ascendency, health and well-being, and an ever-expanding sphere of influence. Yes, by that definition, Paul is living in denial.

That's the very definition, though, that has us all in trouble. It's the definition that gives pastors and presidents credibility issues because it cares about the results they produce while turning a blind eye to the character (or lack thereof) they display. It's the definition that adds fuel to the fires of idolatry named "success" and "upward mobility." It's even the reason there's a reactionary caricature of triumph that presumes it's only available for the impoverished, oppressed, and outcasts. Our bad definition of triumph is at the core of our restlessness, and it's one of the reasons it has taken me two years to finish writing this book.

"Triumph," says Paul, *"is smelling like Jesus."* Nothing more. Nothing less. Nothing else. A life of triumph is a life in which the aromas of love, joy, peace, patience, kindness, goodness, faithfulness, gentleness, and self-control are wafting through the air, flowing from the pores of our daily, sometimes mundane, lives. This aroma can be as evident in a million-dollar mansion as in a tent. You can smell it in a CrossFit gym or an oncology ward, in prison or in the Hilton, among CEOs or servants.

This is nothing new or mysterious to Paul. He says it in different ways in different places throughout his writings. In the book of Galatians he uses a different metaphor when he says that he's like a mother in childbirth, so desperately does he want Christ to be formed in those he loves (Gal. 3:19). When he writes the Romans, he tells them that God's design from the very beginning was that God's people would be "conformed to the image of His Son," which is just another way of saying that God's desire is that we all smell like Jesus. If all the meetings, Bible studies, church-life, ministries, and spiritual disciplines I'm engaged in don't lead to my displaying the character of Christ in greater clarity, I've missed the point. It's all a waste of time.

Why Does This Definition of Triumph Instill Hope?

Paul's counterintuitive definition of triumph instills hope because it has brought me a lasting recovery of the perspective I offered in the previous two chapters. In my chapter "Last Tour," I said that it's enough to believe that God will be with me in the future and will express life through me. In "Solitude," I posited that there isn't a single reason in the world for me to be afraid or anxious if I believe what I teach—that Christ is radically present for us, living in union with us as a groom with his bride. We're filled, in other words, with the seeds of his life, and his life is wholeness, joy, strength—in short, all we need.

Retrospectively, I can see it; I can see that the seeds of transformation sown in my sabbatical were indeed sown. But seeds take time to germinate, and in our age of instant gratification, I'd somehow presumed that the simple act of trekking would change me, that the tan and strong legs would indicate an equally profound transformation of heart and soul. Ah, but inner work is slow, and there's a sense in which it's not even work, any more than a seed works to bring forth fruit.

The "work"—if we can say it that way—resides in learning to abide. I thought I'd come home and have, inherent in me by virtue of being physically stronger, a greater capacity to handle stress. I would be more fully present in tense situations, more patient with those whose ways and ideas differ from mine, more generous with my time. It turns out that none of these things came about as a byproduct of exercising in the mountains for days on end.

Rather, the real work of bringing to fruition the seeds planted on our trek would come through the living of real life. Since the sabbatical, we've sold our house, moved to the mountains, incorporated my mother-in-law into our household permanently, incorporated our daughter, son-in-law, and new granddaughter into our household for a year, celebrated our youngest daughter's marriage, hired two new teaching pastors and a new executive pastor, executed a funding campaign to finish a major building project, and restructured the organization of our growing church. In the middle of it all, I've pondered my own future, seeking to discern how best to use the gifts God has given me as I move into what I've titled "the final third" of life. My pondering, though, often led to more anxiety than peace because the "final third" language sounds so very final! This is a "growing old" problem that nobody warned me about.

The lessons I'm learning and the transformation that is occurring isn't happening because I went hiking. Remember the earlier truth about the map not being the journey? It turns out that the journey through the Alps was itself only a map—the real journey would begin on my return home, because it's here that I would make real the principles discovered on the trek, principles that would help me rest in God's goal of increasingly manifesting the aroma of Christ.

Principle #1—Control Is an Illusion

We knew this principle on the hike. We had no control over the weather, the lodging, whether or not they'd have the particular kinds of foods we'd enjoy on the certain night we were in a hut, whether we'd enjoy the luxury of a private room or be stacked in the "lagger" five or six across, with another dozen in the room too, creating a snoring orchestra. Over time, we learned to roll with it and simply enjoy the experience that was served up each and every day. We quickly learned that our expectations, should they not be met, created a sort of "double penalty." We were both upset about the thing ("Why did they give us a private room, and then when we return from dinner we find a couple asleep in our bed!?" Yes, this happened) and upset about our inflamed response to the thing ("Why am I overreacting! Why can't I be calm! Why are there people in our bed!"). Once we surrendered our addiction to the illusion of control, every day became an opportunity to adapt and to find joy in other things rather than to fixate on our disappointments.

Here at home, though, I quickly fell back into the pursuit of that elusive space where everything goes "according to plan." The instances of this flaw are too numerous and too personal to recount. Suffice it to say, I quickly fell into the trap of believing that with enough planning and effort, I could build my future, customized and all lived out according to my ambitions and desires. This created expectations—expectations that often were dashed—and this would send me into a space of introspection, asking myself what I'd done wrong. The reality, seen with greater clarity through the passing of time, is that I'd done nothing wrong other than demand of God that people, plans, and events in my life unfold according to my plans and timetable. It's as if I had a script in mind for my days, and I'd get upset with either God or myself for messing it up when things didn't work right. The problem? I'm not intended to be the author of the story. I need to relax and let things ripen in due time. It seems silly now, looking back, but it set me up for more anxiety than I'd ever experienced, because my post-sabbatical life had more variables and elements outside of my control than I'd ever experienced before.

Peace has come, though, as the sabbatical seeds have matured. I've had the chance to learn the principles just articulated in the "Solitude" chapter. God has never promised us immunity from the effects of living in a fallen world. We'll face our share of disease, loss, betrayal, financial setbacks. So to the extent that we seek to live what I call a "bombproof" life, we actually end up sabotaging the good life for which we're created. You can put millions in the bank, maybe. But you can't control mutant cells, and cancer still takes your spouse, or you. Or reverse that. You're blessed with good health, but you never come to the point of saying, like the foolish farmer who is the role model for so many of us, "This is what I will do: I will tear down my barns and build larger ones, and there I will store all my grain and my goods. And I will say to my soul, 'Soul, you have many goods laid up for many years to come; take your ease . . .'" (Luke 12:18–19). Of course, Jesus says in the very next sentence that the farmer's priorities were completely wrong.

Control? It's an illusion. What God has promised us is not insulation, or magic protection from the results of the Fall. God has promised us Presence, and remarkably, has promised that the Presence will be enough—just what we need to live a life of peace, joy, hope, rest. We learned to rest on our journey when we dropped our expectations of what would happen on any given day and simply enjoyed the day for what it would bring us. I'm learning, slowly, to do the same in real life.

This isn't blind optimism or denial. Rather, it's planning prayerfully and then, once we have committed our plans to Christ, having the faith and courage to believe that what unfolds is allowed by God and that God will give us the resources to walk through it, come what may. The result, as I've slowly learned to apply this, has been more rest, peace, and confidence that even though I don't know the future and can't even seem to plan it due to all the variables, I do know who will be walking with me. That, it turns out, is all I need to know.

Principle #2—Transformation Happens Slowly and Passively

Trekking day after day changes the body, inevitably. It's a cause-and-effect thing, having to do with mitochondria, adaptation to stress, cardio capacity, and more, as we've seen. You don't will your way into greater cardio capacity just by telling your heart to be strong. You don't will your way into greater muscle strength just by reading about muscle development and mentally affirming your new knowledge. Why then do we think that we can will ourselves to joy, or patience, or generosity, as if we could develop an eight-week program for "joy," forcing it to come into existence?

It's not that we have nothing to do, no role to play. Rather, it's that our role is what I call "soil development of the soul." I say this partly because of the marvelous "soil truths" offered in Mark 4. In essence Jesus likens our process of transformation to the mystery of how a seed grows in soil. In one parable he straight out tells us that the growth is a mystery. A man casts his seed in the soil, and then "he goes to bed at night and gets up by day, and the seed sprouts and grows—how, he himself does not know" (Mark 4:27). Our transformation is a mystery.

In this mystery of transformation, though, you and I have things we must do. Your heart and muscles aren't transformed without exercise; and likewise, your life in Christ will never be transformed without active "soil care." This is shown to us in the other Mark 4 parable, where we learn that some seeds are choked from growth by alien elements in the soil: worries of the world, the deceitfulness of riches, the desires for other things. Jesus also mentions certain aversions that become barriers—fear of persecution and affliction, for example. So there you have it. Our job is soil-care, which we accomplish by leaning into the suffering that comes our way and welcoming trials and challenges as a context in which Christ can be more fully shaped in us. It's right here that I've been able to apply some of the lessons learned on our trek. When I was hungry, tired, or hot, two things helped me press forward.

First, I knew that pressing forward was producing greater capacity in my body, that this was the very context in which I was being transformed for the better. This is precisely why James tells us in his letter to consider it "pure joy" when we encounter various trials.[2] Such trials, he goes on to say, are the context in which "endurance" is produced. It's not that we're grateful for the suffering or the challenge; it's that we've learned through experience that what James says is true— the suffering and challenge are a context that enriches the soil so that the seed of Christ's life can grow and thrive. We're being weaned from our addiction to accolades, creature comforts, and a predictable life, and this is making us more like Christ—wiser, more patient, gentler. What's not to like about that? Yet, the only path for such transformation is the path of hardship, the path that cuts across our desires. Acceptance of hard times and tasks will be the way forward.

The second thing that helped me to endure while on the trail was the practice of gratitude. On days when snow made my feet cold or steep climbs challenged my Achilles, I was sustained by giving thanks for things in the environment, little artistries received as gifts from the Creator: a stunning blossom peeking through the snow, a high peak turning a riot of color in the alpenglow of sunset, mountain goats feasting. A foundational truth learned on my trek and now applied daily in real life is that there's always a cause for gratitude. Now when I'm parked on the freeway that is Seattle traffic, I'm more inclined to give thanks for the gift of having a car, or for the beauty of the city I live in, or the mountains on the horizon, or the people in their cars, each with longings, each with a story.

The byproduct of responding well to the journey of our daily lives is that the soil of our hearts slowly yet relentlessly is being purified and fortified. Good soil means good fruit, so, instead of continually introspecting and wondering if we're good enough, joyful enough, holy enough, we can rest confidently, knowing that our transformation is occurring. Relax. Respond to the journey with gratitude and endurance. Know that God is shaping you to be a unique expression of Christ.

To the extent that I've applied them, these simple truths have served me well in the days since we came home, as uncertainties, challenges, and change in many ways have become the norm more than the exception. I'm learning to rest confidently in the truth that the scent of hope, generosity, peace, joy, wisdom, holiness, and wholeness that is Christ will be increasingly evident in my life as long as I continue to do a little soil-care and continue receiving his seed. It won't happen according to my timetable. It won't look like I think it should look. But it will happen, little by little, and knowing this is good enough to give me peace and rest.

Principle #3—The Journey *Is* the Destination

September 19, 2014. Güttenberghaus. *(Taken directly from Donna's journal.) Woke up to perfectly clear skies. The stars during the night were beautiful and, as if on cue, God gave us a display of shooting stars as well. From this vantage point we can look out over Ramsau, Vorberg, and Schladming, and marvel at how this corner of the world has also become* *our home over the years. We don't yet know the full story of our future, but we're so very grateful for the chapters which include our Austrian family. We wrestled with hiking farther, but last night was such an excellent time of closure that it just felt right to make our way down, but not until we hiked "just up around the bend to see what's beyond." That's such a Richard-thing to do, always looking ahead to see what's next. The view around the corner was both beautiful and tempting, but it's time to go home.*

Yes, it's true. I'm still eager to see what's around the corner. There's a difference, though, between how I did that looking two years ago and my looking now. In the past, the looking ahead was motivated by a strange blend of vision, curiosity, and anxiety, and if the truth be told, anxiety was often the main ingredient. I mirrored exactly what Jesus talks about in his most famous sermon when he says, "Do not worry about your life as to what you will eat or what you will drink; nor for your body as to what you will put on." Ah, but I have worried. I've worried because I've listened to the voices telling me that I'm on my own, and that on my own, I'm not nearly enough to make it. They're there, those voices, hidden in the recesses of my soul, poisoning trust, stealing rest, sabotaging peace.

Donna continues in her journal from the Güttenberghaus: "There are still many questions about our future, but this journey has shown us that our plans can be completely altered and turn out so much better when held openly so that God can direct our steps."

Indeed, this is the most profound lesson my trek taught me. For me, the gap between mind and experience has closed because of this trek, and my hope and prayer are that nuggets of truth discovered and shared here will help others close the gap too.

November 18, 2016. Cabin in the Sierra Nevada Mountains. *The power was out in the cabin until after dark last night, so I scrounged some wood and will now light a fire in the fireplace to gain a little heat. This precious space is dark, quiet, cold. The silence is broken by the striking of a match. Then, light! The paper receives the flame and begins burning. I add toilet paper (the only burnable paper I can find in the cabin), and soon I hear the crackle of small sticks. Sound! Fire gives birth to fire, and soon the stone fireplace is full of dancing, crackling, vibrant flames. The room is lit, and warmth begins to emanate outward, filling me, blessing me.*

"This is your calling, Richard," I hear. "The light of the world. The world is cold and dark, disillusioned by politics, fearful of terror, lonely and isolated, shattered by addictions. You, and all my people, must rise to your calling. Be light. Be warmth. Be inviting." I'm awed by awareness of a Presence, always there in reality but rarely perceived with clarity. I often don't want such a calling, but in this moment, shivering still with cold, I pray. "Thank you," is all I say as light from the fire fills the room. Underneath the vast awareness of my inadequacy, there's a realization that it's Christ's light, not mine, that is the source of this calling. For this reason, I can receive it. So can you.

This morning I wake to a warm cabin, with power restored, and I brew some coffee for my time of meeting with Christ. I read, pray, journal a bit, and then begin meditating on Psalm 23, that priceless text that explains my relationship with God as that of a sheep to its shepherd. By meditating, I simply mean sitting quietly with my eyes closed and praying each line slowly, letting the words sink in, visualizing the imagery, and letting other intrusive thoughts pass away as I continually return to the text.

I've been praying this prayer, meditating on this psalm, for about a month now, and I have the sense that it will be my companion for at least the rest of the year. It's so rich, so healing, so life-giving. I can't get enough.

This morning, a phrase tears my soul open: "Surely goodness and loving kindness will follow me all the days of my life."

"All the days of my life." Images flood my soul, like the trailer for a movie entitled God's Been Good. *There I am, being adopted, chosen by parents who, though far from perfect, will give me great gifts of love. There I am at the graveside of my dad, not knowing how I'll make it without him. There I am two years later, depressed and lonely, when, in these very mountains, I'm invited to make knowing God my chief aim in life. There I am at the end of seminary, being redirected by God from my plans to be a teacher in a college to God's plans for pastoral ministry. There I am, saying yes to urban ministry, in spite of my own desires, my own mis-givings. All the while, I can see it now—"goodness and loving kindness have been with me."*

The details of my future, as a sixty-year-old, are still uncertain. But as I inhale the truth that God's goodness and mercy have been with me, and will be with me, all the days of my life, I'm able to exhale anxiety and say yes to walking with God into the future, whatever it may hold. I can know that the Shepherd will be with me, that the Light will shine through me with greater clarity, and the scent of Jesus will grow. And because of this, I'm not only at peace, I know I'll be at peace, come what may. I know this because the where, the how, the what, no longer matter so much to me. All those concerns have been displaced by the certitude and promise of "the Who." Knowing the Shepherd will walk with me all the days of my life? That's enough. I smile, realizing that the faith I once had has become not as real as it once was, but more real than ever, for having walked the Alps.

It's time to pack and head home to the future.

Donna's Packing List

- Black Diamond Trekking poles
- Osprey Tempest 40 backpack with 3L hydration bladder and waterproof pack cover
- REI Travel Sack sleeping bag
- compression stuff sack for clothing
- breathable/waterproof rain parka
- lightweight tiny umbrella
- Solomon hiking boots
- Luna sandals
- ankle gaiters (for occasional snow or to keep socks clean on muddy trails)
- down jacket
- Patagonia Nano-Puff jacket
- 2 long-sleeve wicking pullover shirts (keep one for after shower only)
- Long-sleeve button-up tech shirt w/ UV protection
- Long-sleeve lightweight fleece
- 2 wicking tank tops (keep one clean for after shower only)
- 2 quick-dry sports bras
- 3 quick-dry underpants
- 2 pair wool blend socks
- 2 pair nylon sock liners
- hiking pants (zip-off legs eliminate need for extra shorts)
- hiking skirt (for warm days or to look nice in town)
- hiking tights (for extra warmth under pants or with hiking skirt)
- knit gloves
- warm hat (that covers ears)
- baseball cap or wide brim hat for sun
- bandana
- quick-dry towel

- sunglasses and sunscreen
- first-aid kit containing: band-aids, moleskin, blister bandages, Neosporin, throat lozenges, Airborne, anti-inflammatory pills, electrolyte powder
- tiny sewing repair kit
- Swiss Army knife with scissors and tweezers
- headlamp with red-light setting for use inside lagers (communal hut dorm rooms)
- toiletries: shampoo, soap, comb, hair ties, nail clippers, toothbrush and paste, lotion

Notes

[1] The wise old man from *The Lord of the Rings* by J. R. R. Tolkien. He embodies servant-leadership, wisdom, and strength in old age.

[2] James 1:2.

CPSIA information can be obtained
at www.ICGtesting.com
Printed in the USA
FFOW05n0632061217